William Wordsworth

General directions for the
Printer.

These two Volumes are to be printed uniform with the Lyrical
Ballads. in a stanza of four lines, four stanzas in a page; the
first page of each Poem only printing 2 or 3 stanzas according
to the length of the Title — In a Poem the stanzas of which are 5 lines, 3 stanzas
in a Page, with like allowance for the beginning — where the stanzas are
6 lines likewise 3 stanzas in a Page — where 7 — two & a half stanzas
in a Page — where 8 only 2 stanzas in a Page — 9 & 10 two
also — In Couplets or Blank Verse 19 lines in each Page. &
NB This will imply that the stanzas must never be broken into
different Pages, except where there are in one instance
&7 lines in a stanza. And I will
thank you to be as speedy with
the work as possible. You
shall be regularly supplied
with Copy. I will send a sheet
by the next Post. —

The following Note must be inserted
at the end of the Poem which stands
last in this Sheet "Character of the happy
Warrior"]

Note

The above Verses were written soon
after tidings had been received of the
death of Lord Nelson, which event
directed the Author's thoughts to the
subject. His respect for the memory
of his great fellow-countryman induced
him to mention this; though he is
well aware that the Verses must
suffer from any connection in the
Reader's mind with a Name so
illustrious.

To the small Celandine.
(Common Pilewort
or the foilfoot of Scotch)

To the small Celandine.
(Common Pilewort)

Pansies, Lillies, Kingcups, Daisies,
Let them live upon their praises;
Long as there's a sun that sets
Primroses will have their glory;
Long as there are Violets,
They will have a place in story:
There's a flower that shall be mine,
'Tis the little Celandine.

Eyes of some men travel far
For the finding of a star;
Up and down the heavens they go,
Men that keep a mighty rout!
I'm as great as they, I trow,
Since the day I found thee out,
Little flower! — I'll make a stir
Like a great Astronomer.

Modest, yet withal an Elf
Bold, and lavish of thyself,
Since we needs must first have met
I have seen thee, high and low,
Thirty years or more, and yet
'Twas a face I did not know;
Thou hast now, go where I may,
Fifty greetings in a day.

THE BRITISH LIBRARY
writers' lives

William Wordsworth

STEPHEN HEBRON

OXFORD
UNIVERSITY PRESS

DOVE COTTAGE
· Wordsworth Cottage ·
Tickets are available from the shop

❧ Contents

7   **COCKERMOUTH & HAWKSHEAD: 1770–87**

16   **CAMBRIDGE: 1787–91**

24   **FRANCE: 1791–92**

28   **LONDON: 1792–95**

34   **RACEDOWN: 1795–97**

39   **ALFOXDEN: 1797–98**

49   **GERMANY & THE NORTH EAST: 1798–99**

55   **DOVE COTTAGE: 1799–1801**

62   **DOVE COTTAGE: 1801–5**

74   **DOVE COTTAGE: 1805–8**

81   **GRASMERE: 1808–13**

88   **RYDAL MOUNT: 1813–15**

94   **RYDAL MOUNT: 1816–20**

101 **RYDAL MOUNT 1821–32**

107 **RYDAL MOUNT 1833–50**

114 **CHRONOLOGY**

117 **FURTHER READING**

118 **INDEX**

Map showing places in England associated with Wordsworth and his friends and family.

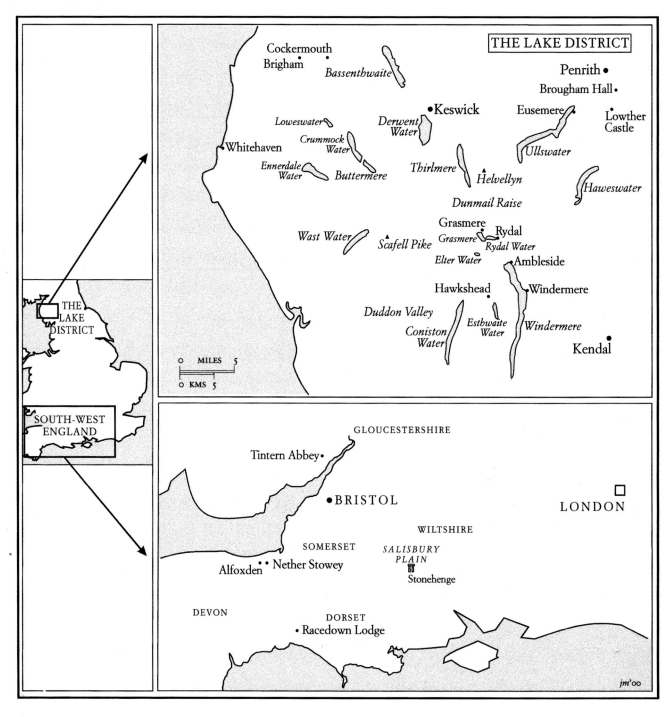

THE LAKE DISTRICT

Cockermouth
Brigham
Bassenthwaite

Penrith
Brougham Hall

Keswick
Derwent Water
Eusemere
Lowther Castle

Loweswater
Crummock Water
Whitehaven
Ullswater

Ennerdale Water
Buttermere
Thirlmere
Helvellyn
Haweswater

Dunmail Raise

Grasmere
Rydal

Wast Water
Scafell Pike
Grasmere
Rydal Water
Elter Water
Ambleside

Hawkshead
Windermere

Duddon Valley
Esthwaite Water
Windermere

Coniston Water
Kendal

MILES 5
KMS 5

GLOUCESTERSHIRE

Tintern Abbey

BRISTOL
LONDON

WILTSHIRE

SOMERSET
SALISBURY PLAIN
Alfoxden Nether Stowey
Stonehenge

DEVON
DORSET
Racedown Lodge

THE LAKE DISTRICT

SOUTH-WEST ENGLAND

jm'00

Cockermouth and Hawkshead: 1770–87

William Wordsworth was born on 7 April 1770 in Cockermouth, a small market town in the north-west corner of the English Lake District. He was the second son of John Wordsworth, a lawyer, and Ann Cookson. An elder brother, Richard, had been born two years earlier. His only sister, Dorothy, was born in 1771, and after her came two younger brothers, John in 1772, and Christopher in 1774.

Wordsworth always considered himself fortunate in his birthplace. For as a child in Cockermouth, he grew up around nature. His earliest memory was the gentle voice of the Derwent, 'the fairest of all rivers', that ran along the bottom of the garden, and which 'loved / To blend his murmurs with my nurse's song'. Later, as a five year-old, he would go swimming in the river, and make 'one long bathing of a summer's day'. At other times he would run 'Over the sandy fields, leaping through groves / Of yellow grunsel', or, 'alone / Beneath the sky', would 'run abroad in wantonness, to sport, / A naked Savage, in the thunder shower'.

Life did, however, have its darker side. Wordsworth's father worked as an attorney for Sir James Lowther, then the wealthiest, most powerful man in that part of England, and was often away from home touring his employer's vast estates. This may explain why Wordsworth, his brothers and sister were frequently sent to stay with their maternal grandparents, William and Dorothy Cookson, in nearby Penrith. Wordsworth hated these visits, so different from the freedom of Cockermouth. 'I was of a stiff, moody and violent temper', he later recalled, 'so much so that I remember going once into the attics of my grandfather's house at Penrith, upon some indignity having been put upon me, with an intention of destroying myself with one of the foils which I knew was kept there. I took the foil in hand, but my heart failed.'

There was another, unforgettable episode at Penrith. One day Wordsworth and a servant, 'Honest James', rode out towards the Beacon, a signal stone on the summit of a hill above the town. The two became separated, and, dismounting,

Wordsworth led his horse over the bleak landscape and down into a quarry. This was, he suddenly realized, the spot where a murderer had once been executed, and in his mind he imagined the gallows, and the body of the murderer swinging in his iron case. Climbing out of the quarry in fright, he came upon a 'naked pool', and, before it, a girl with a pitcher on her head, struggling against the wind:

Opposite page:

Wordsworth's birthplace in Cockermouth, Cumbria, as it is today.

The National Trust Photographic Library/ Magnus Reid

> *It was, in truth,*
> *An ordinary sight, but I should need*
> *Colours and words that are unknown to man*
> *To paint the visionary dreariness*
> *Which, while I looked all round for my lost guide,*
> *Did at that time invest the naked pool,*
> *The beacon on the lonely eminence,*
> *The woman, and her garments vexed and tossed*
> *By the strong wind.*

There were many such events in Wordsworth's childhood – 'spots of time' he came to call them. In his imagination, he transformed these outwardly unremarkable events into moments of emotional intensity and lasting power.

In 1778, shortly before Wordsworth's eighth birthday, everything changed. At the beginning of the year his mother went to London to visit a friend. There she became ill, apparently after sleeping in a damp bed, and less than two months later she was dead. 'Early died / My honoured mother', Wordsworth wrote many years later, 'she who was the heart / And hinge of all our learnings and our love'. With her death, the existence that he knew and loved at Cockermouth came to an end. Dorothy, his constant friend and companion, was sent to live with cousins in Halifax, a hundred miles away in Yorkshire. They were not to see each other again for nine years. Then, in May 1779, he and his brother Richard were sent to the grammar school at Hawkshead, a village thirty miles to the south, in the heart of the Lake District.

If Wordsworth considered himself lucky to have been born at Cockermouth, then he was, he knew, no less fortunate in where he went to school, 'that beloved

Vale to which, erelong, / I was transplanted'. Hawkshead village lies at the head of Esthwaite Water, one of the region's smaller lakes. Tourists were just beginning to come to the Lake District in large numbers, but in 1779 Esthwaite remained a secluded spot, overlooked in favour of its more spectacular neighbours, Windermere to the east, and Coniston to the west. Its inhabitants formed a close, industrious community. They were farmers, labourers and shepherds, builders and joiners, blacksmiths, bakers and shopkeepers. The unassuming dignity of these 'plain living people' – 'the quiet woodman in the woods, / The shepherd on the hills' – made a deep impression on the young Wordsworth.

Hawkshead Grammar School had been founded in 1585 by Edwin Sandys, an Archbishop of York. With more than a hundred boarders it was a good sized school, and had a fine reputation. Wordsworth and his brother Richard took lodgings with Hugh Tyson, a joiner, and his wife Ann, a grocer and draper. The Tysons kept a cottage first in Hawkshead, and then, after 1783, in the adjoining

hamlet of Colthouse, and for eight years were to provide Wordsworth with a stable and loving home. He remembered Ann Tyson, his 'grey-haired Dame', with particular affection, lovingly recalling her 'smooth domestic life', her 'little daily growth / Of calm enjoyments', and how, on Sunday afternoons, she would fall asleep over her Bible. 'The thoughts of gratitude shall fall like dew / Upon thy grave, good creature', he later wrote, 'while my heart / Can beat I never will forget thy name'.

Hawkshead gave Wordsworth ample opportunity to indulge his delight in outdoor pursuits. Sometimes these were solitary: he would 'wander half the night

Sir James Lowther, Wordsworth's father's employer. 'Truly a madman', said one contemporary, 'but too rich to be confined.' Portrait by Thomas Hudson from c.1755.

among the cliffs' hunting woodcocks, or rise early in the morning, climb the fell and look out over the silent, sleeping valley. At other times he would join his fellow pupils in 'games confederate': in the summer they went boating on Windermere and Coniston; in the winter, they skated on Esthwaite. Occasionally they went further afield, riding out to the ruins of Furness Abbey twenty miles away, then galloping home over Cartmel Sands.

But much of Wordsworth's time was, of course, spent in the classroom. In the summer, lessons began at six or six-thirty in the morning, and lasted until eleven; they recommenced at one o'clock and ran until five. During the winter these hours were slightly shorter. The curriculum concentrated on those subjects essential for future academic success – Latin and Greek, mathematics and science – but Wordsworth was also encouraged to read literature. At Cockermouth his father had urged him to learn 'large portions of Shakespeare and Milton' by heart. Now, at Hawkshead, he had teachers who could build upon this foundation. His first headmaster, William Taylor, 'loved the poets', and Taylor's successor, the Reverend Thomas Bowman, introduced him to modern literature: James Beattie's *The Minstrel*, William Cowper's *The Task*, Percy's *Reliques*, and Robert Burns's *Poems, Chiefly in the Scottish Dialect*. Wordsworth read all he could; he was, Bowman's son recollected, 'one of the very few boys, who used to read the old books in the school library'.

He was also encouraged to write. Taylor gave him some formal exercises to do – verses on 'the summer vacation', a hundred lines to celebrate the bicentenary of the school's foundation – and before long he was writing of his own accord. It was at this time, Wordsworth later said, that he first became 'open to the charm / Of words in tuneful order, found them sweet / *For their own sakes* – a passion and a power'.

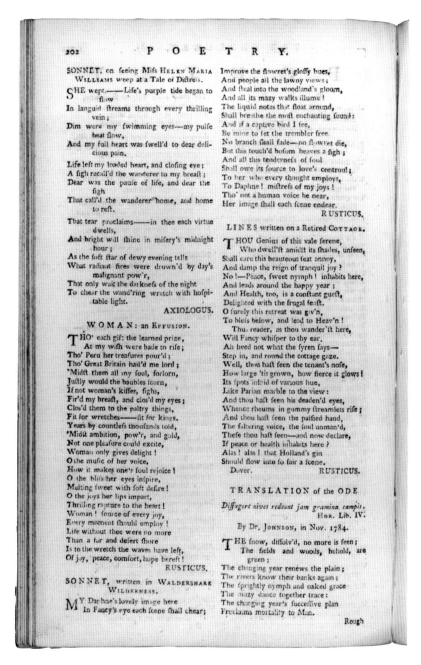

Wordsworth's first published poem, 'Sonnet, on seeing Miss Helen Maria Williams weep at a Tale of Distress', appeared in the European Magazine in March 1787. The signature, 'Axiologus', is a Latin rendering of his own name.

The British Library, PP5459 z

In the middle of Wordsworth's fourth year at Hawkshead his life was again hit by domestic tragedy. In 1783, he returned to Cockermouth as usual for Christmas, only to find his father seriously ill. John Wordsworth had got lost one evening on his way back home, and been forced to spend the night in the open. Less than a fortnight later he was dead, and Wordsworth and his brothers, now

A surviving fragment of 'The Vale of Esthwaite', the poem Wordsworth composed shortly before he went to Cambridge in 1787.

Wordsworth Trust

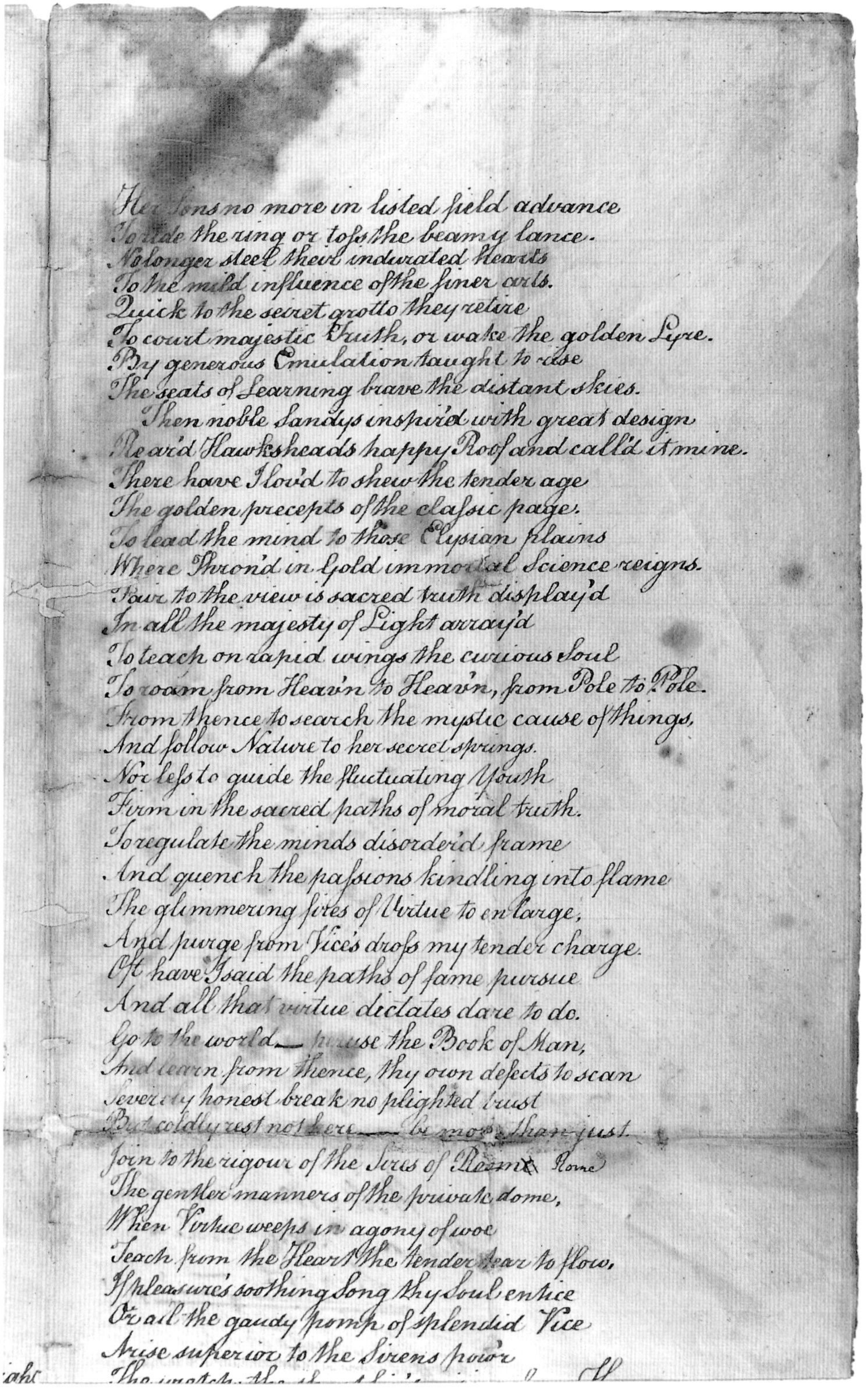

Her sons no more in listed field advance
To ride the ring or toss the beamy lance.
No longer steel their indurated hearts
To the mild influence of the finer arts.
Quick to the secret grotto they retire
To court majestic Truth, or wake the golden Lyre.
By generous Emulation taught to rise
The seats of Learning brave the distant skies.
Then noble Sandys inspir'd with great design
Rear'd Hawksheads happy Roof and call'd it mine.
There have I lov'd to shew the tender age
The golden precepts of the classic page.
To lead the mind to those Elysian plains
Where Thron'd in Gold immortal Science reigns.
Fair to the view is sacred truth display'd
In all the majesty of Light array'd
To teach on rapid wings the curious Soul
To roam from Heav'n to Heav'n, from Pole to Pole.
From thence to search the mystic cause of things,
And follow Nature to her secret springs.
Nor less to guide the fluctuating Youth
Firm in the sacred paths of moral truth.
To regulate the minds disorder'd frame
And quench the passions kindling into flame
The glimmering fires of Virtue to enlarge,
And purge from Vice's dross my tender charge.
Oft have I said the paths of fame pursue
And all that virtue dictates dare to do.
Go to the world — peruse the Book of Man,
And learn from thence, thy own defects to scan
Severely honest break no plighted trust
But coldly rest not here — be more than just.
Join to the rigour of the Sires of Rome
The gentler manners of the private dome,
When Virtue weeps in agony of woe
Teach from the Heart the tender tear to flow,
If pleasure's soothing Song thy Soul entice
Or all the gaudy pomp of splendid Vice
Arise superior to the Sirens pow'r

orphans, 'Followed his body to the grave'. From now on the children were in the care of their legal guardians: Richard Wordsworth, their father's brother, in Whitehaven, and Christopher Crackanthorpe Cookson, their mother's brother, in Penrith. Christmases, spent at Whitehaven, were bearable, but summer holidays in Penrith became something to dread. Christopher Cookson, 'Uncle Kit', seems to have got on particularly badly with Wordsworth. To make matters worse, it became clear that on his death, Wordsworth's father had been owed over four thousand pounds by Sir James Lowther, now the first Earl of Lonsdale. A bill for this amount was sent, but the Earl refused even to acknowledge it. The resulting lawsuit between the Wordsworths and 'Wicked Jimmy' was to drag on for years.

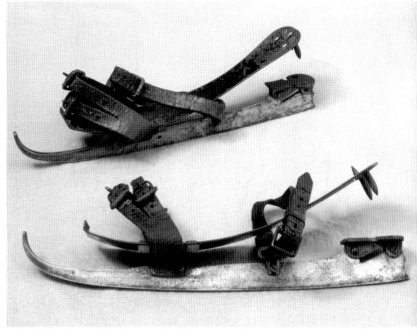

Wordsworth's ice-skates. Skating on Esthwaite Water in winter was a favourite pastime during Wordsworth's childhood, and even in his sixties he was described as 'the crack skater on Rydal Lake'.

Wordsworth Trust

Wordsworth spent a further two and a half years at Hawkshead after his father's death. His final year, 1787, was a memorable one. In March, he became a published poet – a coventional sonnet, 'On hearing Miss Helen Maria Williams weep at a Tale of Distress', appeared in the *European Magazine* under the pseudonym 'Axiologus'. He also embarked upon his first long poem, 'The Vale of Esthwaite', of which only fragments now survive. Then, in June, 'after separation desolate', he was at last reunited with Dorothy at Penrith. Together with a childhood friend, Mary Hutchinson, they explored the countryside around the River Emont, spending many hours among the ruins of Brougham Castle, where they would lie on the ground, 'listening to the wild-flowers and the grass / As they gave out their whispers to the wind'. But the reunion was all too brief. At the end of October brother and sister were again separated, when Wordsworth left Penrith for the south, and Cambridge University.

Cambridge: 1787-91

The first Wordsworth saw of Cambridge was the outline of King's College Chapel rising out of the flat fenland landscape. Then a student, 'clothed in gown and tasselled cap', passed his coach, and he watched, fascinated, until 'he was left a hundred yards behind'. Entering the city, Wordsworth passed the castle, crossed the River Cam by Magdalene Bridge, and disembarked at the Hoop Inn. That first day he enrolled as a member of St John's College, and took possession of his new rooms. They were humble enough – directly above the college kitchens, and with a bedroom that was little more than a closet – but from his window he could see Trinity College Chapel and Roubiliac's famous statue of Isaac Newton.

During his first weeks at Cambridge Wordsworth's spirits were high. The unfamiliar sights and sounds of the ancient university city enthralled him:

I was the Dreamer, they the Dream; I roamed
Delighted, through the motley spectacle;
Gowns grave or gaudy, Doctors, Students, Streets,
Lamps, Gateways, Flocks of Churches, Courts and Towers:
Strange transformation for a mountain Youth,
A northern Villager.

He also began well academically, scoring highly in his initial examinations. But the strong sense of rootedness he had known at Cockermouth and Hawkshead was not to be repeated at Cambridge. Before long, his sense of purpose started to weaken, and, once 'the first glitter of the show was passed', his mind 'returned into its former self'. The reasons for this were several. There was his disillusionment with the drunken, sometimes riotous behaviour of the undergraduates, and his deep distrust of competitive examinations. He was also reacting against the weight of expectation put on him by his relatives. His uncle, William Cookson, confidently expected Wordsworth to sit for an honours degree and become, like him, a senior member of St John's College, or failing that, a lawyer like his father. Neither prospect appealed to Wordsworth. His overriding feeling was he was 'not for that hour / Nor for that place'; he was 'ill-tutored for captivity', and wanted to experiment, to pursue a course of study that had 'an ampler range / And freer pace'. So, 'detached / Internally from academic cares', he explored the Cambridgeshire countryside, and read widely. He engaged a private tutor to teach him Italian, and made his own translations of Virgil. Above all, he deepened his already considerable knowledge of the English poets.

Significantly, for his first two summer vacations, in 1788 and 1789, Wordsworth left Cambridge and headed straight for Hawkshead. This was still his real home, and he found himself greeting old friends 'doubtless with a little pride / But more with shame, for my habiliments, / The transformation, and the gay attire'. While in the north he also paid brief visits to his guardians at Whitehaven and Penrith, but they were made more out of courtesy than anything else. 'I should have been happy if he had favoured me with more of his Company', Christopher Cookson wrote to Wordsworth's elder brother Richard, now a lawyer, in 1789, 'but I'm afraid

William Wordsworth

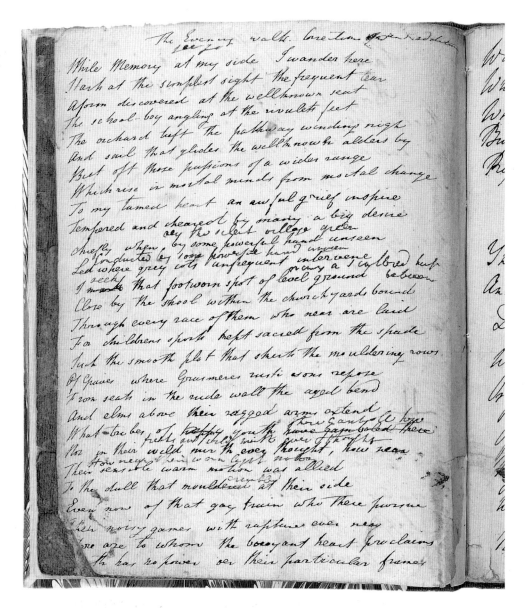

I'm out of his good graces.' He was also writing – not, to his uncle's chagrin, verses he had been invited to compose to commemorate the death of the Master of St John's that year, but a long poem, *An Evening Walk*, addressed to Dorothy and celebrating the beauties of his native landscape.

For his final summer vacation, however, Wordsworth was altogether more ambitious. On 13 July 1790 he and a Cambridge friend from North Wales, Robert Jones, set sail from Dover, bound for France. They landed at Calais that evening, and

An amateur depiction of the fall of the Bastille in Paris, 14 July 1789, made by one of the attackers, Claude Cholat.

Musées de la Ville de Paris

the next morning began a twelve-week walking tour of the continent. 'We went staff in hand', Wordsworth recalled more than fifty years later, 'without knapsacks, and carrying each his needments tied up in a pocket handkerchief, with about twenty pounds apiece in our pockets.' It was an intoxicating time to travel through France, for the country was, as Wordsworth put it in a letter to Dorothy, 'mad with joy in consequence of the revolution'. In May the previous year, King Louis XVI, in an attempt to maintain control over his debt-ridden country, had summoned his parliament, the States-General, but by July had been forced to replace the States-General with a National Assembly, and absolute political power had passed out of the hands of the aristocracy. On 14 July, the Bastille, the Paris fortress which symbolised the old feudal order, had been stormed and destroyed. Wordsworth and Jones were starting their walking tour on the very anniversary of this momentous event, which had come to mark the beginning of the French Revolution. As they left Calais, the Fête de la Fédération was being celebrated in Paris, and the King was swearing an oath of allegiance to the new constitution.

In time, Wordsworth was to follow the course of the Revolution closely and embrace its ideals, but what interested him now was not politics but scenery, specifically, the sublime landscape of the Alps. From Calais he and Jones travelled, on foot and by boat, some five hundred miles south to Lyons. Then they turned east, and by 4 October had reached the mountains around the monastery of the Grande Chartreuse, described by the poet Thomas Gray in 1719 as 'one of the most poetical scenes imaginable'. Here, for the only time on the entire trip, they allowed themselves a day's rest. From the Chartreuse they walked north to Lake Geneva, and then on to the great glaciers of Chamounix, and the Alps' highest peak, Mont Blanc. On 17 August they crossed the Alps over the Simplon Pass, and descended into Italy through the Ravine of Gondo. It was an unforgettable moment, one which years later Wordsworth would magnificently describe in Book VI of *The Prelude*:

> *The immeasurable height*
> *Of woods decaying, never to be decayed,*
> *The stationary blasts of waterfalls,*
> *And everywhere along the hollow rent*
> *Winds thwarting winds, bewildered and forlorn,*
> *The torrents shooting from the clear blue sky,*
> *The rocks that muttered close upon our ears –*
> *Black drizzling crags that spake by the wayside*
> *As if a voice were in them – the sick sight*
> *And giddy prospect of the raving stream …*

At the time, however, all Wordsworth could do was lament his inability to transfer his feelings on to paper: 'this Catalogue must be shockingly tedious', he wrote to Dorothy from Lake Constance. 'Ten thousand times in the course of this tour have I regretted the inability of my memory to retain a more strong impression of the beautiful forms before me, and again and again in quitting a fortunate station have I returned to it with the most lively picture.' But he rightly guessed that his experiences would remain with him: 'When many of these landscapes are floating before my mind', he told Dorothy, 'I felt a high [enjoyment] in reflecting that

A contemporary view of the Alps is depicted in The Passage of the St Gothard *by J.M.W. Turner, 1804.*

Abbot Hall Art Gallery

William Wordsworth

The earliest surviving letter by Wordsworth, written to his sister Dorothy from Lake Constance in September 1790. He describes his journey into Switzerland from the Grande Chartreuse: 'My Spirits have been kept in a perpetual hurry of delight by the almost uninterrupted succession of sublime and beautiful objects which have passed before my eyes during the course of the last month.'

Wordsworth Trust

perhaps scarce a day of my life will pass by [in] which I shall not derive some happiness from these images.'

After crossing the Alps, Wordsworth and Jones walked to the lakes at Maggiore, Lugano and Como, then on to Lake Lucerne and Lake Zurich. From Zurich they travelled along the Rhine to the falls at Schaffhasen. They then proceeded up to Basel, where they bought a boat and navigated down the Rhine to Cologne. They returned to England, via Ostend, on around 11 October. It had been a magnificent achievement. In a little less than three months, Wordsworth and Jones had covered, mostly on foot, almost three thousand miles.

Wordsworth returned for his final term at Cambridge, and in January 1791 graduated with only a pass, rather than a full honours degree. 'William you may have heard lost the chance, indeed the certainty of a fellowship by not combating his inclinations', Dorothy wrote to her Halifax friend Jane Pollard. 'He gave way to his natural dislike of studies so dry as many parts of mathematics, consequently could not succeed at Cambridge. He reads Italian, Spanish, French, Greek and Latin, and English, but never opens a mathematical book.' Wordsworth had little idea what he would do now, and for the next few months whiled away the time while his guardians, on whom he was still financially dependent, tried to persuade him into various careers. They made a number of suggestions – the church, the law, even, at one stage, a professorship in oriental languages – but all without success.

In May, Wordsworth visited Robert Jones at his home, Plas-yn-Llan, in North Wales. It was a much-needed diversion, and Wordsworth remained in Wales for over three months. Between June and August the two friends made another impressive walking tour, this time covering most of North Wales, but Dorothy suspected additional reasons for her brother's prolonged stay: 'Who would not be happy enjoying the company of three young ladies in the Vale of Clewyd', she wrote to Jane Pollard in June, 'and without a rival? His friend Jones is a charming young man; and has *five sisters*, three of whom are at home at present, then there are mountains, rivers, woods and rocks, where charms without any other inducement would be sufficient to tempt William to continue amongst them as long as possible.'

By October Wordsworth was back in London. 'I am doomed to be an idler thro[ughout] my whole life', he confessed to his Cambridge friend William Matthews the following month. 'I have read nothing this age, nor indeed did I ever.' But he had, at least, a plan for the winter: he would go to Orléans, a town just south of Paris, and learn French.

~ *France: 1791–92*

Wordsworth left England on 26 November, and arrived in Dieppe the following day. On 30 November he reached Paris, and spent the next five days sightseeing. He sought out places that had been made famous by the Revolution: Montmartre, a favourite meeting place for revolutionaries; the Field of Mars, where the Fête de la Fédération had been held on 14 July 1790; the Pantheon, now the burial place of Voltaire and Rousseau; the National Assembly; and the Jacobin Club. Walking among the ruins of the Bastille, Wordsworth picked up a piece of rubble as a souvenir. It was a time, he later wrote, 'when Europe was rejoiced, / France standing on the top of golden hours, / And human nature seeming born again', but he could not, as yet, join in the excitement: 'I looked for something I could not find, / Affecting more emotion than I felt'.

On 5 December Wordsworth took the fifty-mile journey south to Orléans. He stayed until early February 1792, then moved on to Blois, a town lying twenty miles to the south east. It was here, finally, that he ceased to look at the Revolution with the detached curiosity of a tourist, and became fully committed to its ideals. In many ways they were ideals he had known and admired all his life. He had, after all, been 'born in a poor district', a place 'of ancient homeliness, / Manners erect, and frank simplicity', and at Hawkshead he had not known anyone who had been 'vested with attention or respect / Through claims of wealth or blood'. Cambridge, too, despite its faults, had been a kind of republic, where 'Distinction lay open to all that came, / And wealth and titles were in less esteem / Than talents or successful industry'. But he needed something to inspire him, to rouse him into real emotional involvement. The friendship he was now to form at Blois provided just the inspiration he required.

Michel Beaupuy, a French army captain, was thirty-six years old, and so fourteen years Wordsworth's senior. Though of noble birth, and a member of a largely Royalist regiment, he was nonetheless a dedicated revolutionary. In the few weeks of their friendship, he was to give Wordsworth some idea of the complicated political events which were then transforming France. Far more importantly, he was a living embodiment of revolutionary principles, a man, Wordsworth later wrote, who 'through the events / Of that great change wandered in perfect faith':

> *Man he loved*
> *As man, and to the mean and the obscure,*
> *And all the homely in their homely works,*
> *Transferred a courtesy which had no air*
> *Of condescension, but did rather seem*
> *A passion and a gallantry, like that*
> *Which he, a soldier, in his idler day*
> *Had payed to woman*

One episode in particular stuck in Wordsworth's mind. One day, he and Beaupuy were walking along the banks of the Loire, and came across a starving girl leading a heifer by a piece of cord. It was a terrible image, and Wordsworth never forgot Beaupuy's reaction:

at the sight my friend
In agitation said, 'Tis against that
Which we are fighting', I with him believed
Devoutly that a spirit was abroad
Which could not be withstood, that poverty,
At least like this, would in a little time
Be found no more …

And so Wordsworth became 'a patriot – and my heart was all / Given to the people, and my love was theirs'. But this was not all. During these intense, vivid months in France, he also became a father.

In Orléans Wordsworth had become intimate with a local girl, Annette Vallon. By September, it was clear that Annette was carrying their child, and the

A miniature thought to be of Annette Vallon, Wordsworth's lover and mother of his first child. Artist unknown.

Wordsworth Trust

following month Wordsworth left for England, seemingly with the intention of raising enough money to enable him to return and marry Annette. By the time their daughter, Caroline, was baptized at Orléans Cathedral on 15 December, he was back in London. Then political events took over, and he found himself unable to return to France: on 1 February 1793, France declared war on England, and safe travel between the two countries became impossible. Wordsworth was not to see Annette and Caroline for another ten years.

Such are the basic facts, but of the emotions and circumstances behind them we know very little. Wordsworth never referred to Annette directly in his poetry, and neither he nor his family ever talked about her at length in their letters or journals. It is only by chance that two letters, written by Annette to Wordsworth and Dorothy in 1793, have survived. Confiscated at the time by the French authorities, they were discovered in 1922. The enduring passion in Annette's anxious words is plain:

> *I would be happier if we were married, but I realize it's almost impossible for you to risk the journey in wartime. You might be taken prisoner. … Come, my love, my husband, accept the kisses of your wife, of your daughter. She is so pretty, this poor little thing, so pretty that if she weren't always in my arms I would go out of my mind. She gets more like you every day …*

London: 1792–95

After his formative experiences in France, Wordsworth now struggled to come to terms with life back in England. The next three years were to be among the most difficult of his life. He had no income, and few intentions. His new-found republicanism made him, in England, an outsider, 'one of that odious class of men called democrats'. In France, he had a daughter who he had never seen.

One of the first things he did was to publish, in January 1793, his two most substantial works to date, *An Evening Walk* and *Descriptive Sketches*. The latter celebrated his 1790 tour of the Alps with Robert Jones, and had mostly been written in Orléans the previous summer. He had little confidence in either of them as poems, but, he told his friend Matthews the following year, 'as I had done nothing by which to distinguish myself at the university, I thought these little things might shew that I could do something'.

His publisher was Joseph Johnson, radical bookseller, and friend and publisher of such prominent Enlightenment figures as Mary Wollstonecraft, William Godwin, Thomas Paine, Joseph Priestley and Erasmus Darwin. With his next work, a political tract, Wordsworth hoped to join this illustrious company. *A Letter to the Bishop of Llandaff* was his reply to Richard Watson, a liberal who, horrified by the execution of Louis XVI in January 1793, had publically abandoned his support of the French Revolution. It showed Wordsworth at his most fiercely republican. He argued for universal suffrage, and with it the abolition of both monarchy and aristocracy. Violence, even the execution of a king, he maintained, was justifiable in the

early stages of a revolution: 'a time of revolution is not the season of true Liberty', he wrote. 'The obstinacy and perversion of men is such that she is too often obliged to borrow the very arms of despotism to overthrow him, and in order to reign in peace must establish herself by violence.'

It was fortunate for Wordsworth that *A Letter to the Bishop of Llandaff* was never, in the end, published. The growing violence of the Revolution, and then the outbreak of war with France, had changed the general mood in England. An alarmed English government sought out revolutionary activity, and suppressed it. Had Wordsworth published his pamphlet he may well have found himself on trial for treason.

In July, Wordsworth spent a month on the Isle of Wight with an old schoolfriend, William Calvert. Every day he would watch, with bitter feelings, the English fleet of Portsmouth preparing itself for the war with France. On the return journey north he parted with Calvert at Salisbury, and spent several days wandering alone over Salisbury Plain. He came upon the prehistoric remains of Stonehenge, and there, introverted and depressed, and 'by the solitude o'ercome', he imagined the savagery of ancient Britain; in his mind the place became a 'sacrificial altar, fed / with living men', and he saw, 'here and there, / A single Briton in his wolf-skin vest / With shield and stone-axe, stride across the Wold'. Shortly afterwards he began 'Salisbury Plain', a bleak poem in which two outcasts, a solitary traveller and a homeless woman, speak of their misfortunes while taking shelter from a storm.

The manuscript of 'Adventures on Salisbury Plain', the poem Wordsworth began shortly after visiting the ruins of Stonehenge in the summer of 1793.

Wordsworth Trust

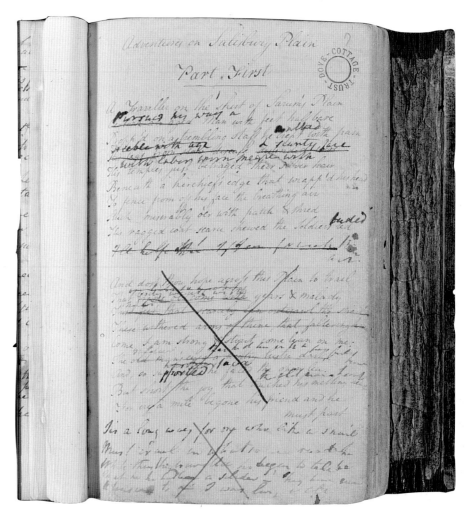

From Salisbury Plain Wordsworth headed north for an old refuge, Robert Jones's home in Wales. He arrived there at the end of August, having taken a route through Bath, Bristol and the Wye Valley, and seems to have stayed with Jones for a little over a month. For the rest of 1793, his movements are uncertain.

'I have been doing nothing, and still continue to be doing nothing', Wordsworth wrote despondently to Matthews in February the following year. 'What is to become of me I know not.' But things were about to improve. That month he was reunited with Dorothy in Halifax, and her company had its usual stabilising influence. 'You can have no idea of my impatience to see this dear Brother', Dorothy had written to Jane Pollard shortly before Wordsworth's arrival. 'Oh count, count the Days ... I measure them with a lover's scale'. The years of separation had done nothing to weaken their old intimacy: 'We have been endeared to each other by early misfortune', Dorothy explained. 'We in the same moment lost a father, a mother, a home, we have been equally deprived of our patrimony by the cruel Hand of lordly Tyranny. These afflictions have all contributed to unite us closer by the Bonds of affection notwithstanding we have been compelled to spend our youth far asunder.' Their fondest wish was that one day they would have a house of their own.

In April Wordsworth and Dorothy went to stay with William Calvert at his home, Windy Brow, near Keswick in the northern part of the Lake District. There Wordsworth revised 'Salisbury Plain' and *An Evening Walk*, and looked after William Calvert's younger brother Raisley, who was dangerously ill with tuberculosis. That autumn, Wordsworth offered to accompany Raisley to Lisbon, thinking that the warm climate would improve Raisley's health. In October they set off, but within hours Raisely's worsening condition forced them to turn back. Twelve weeks later, in January 1795, Raisley died, but not before he had made a remarkable gift; in his will, he had bequeathed Wordsworth the sum of £900. The purpose of this, Wordsworth explained to his brother Richard, was 'to set me above want and to enable me to pursue my literary views or any other views with greater success'. Raisley's bequest, in itself an extraordinary vote of confidence, offered the chance of a life of independence and creative achievement. 'He cleared a passage for me', Wordsworth later wrote, 'and the stream / Flowed in the bent of Nature'.

After Raisley Calvert's death Wordsworth was ready for a change. 'I begin to

wish much to be in town', he had written to Matthews in November. 'Cataracts and mountains, are good for occasional society, but they will not do for constant companions.' By the end of January he was in London, and there, for the first time, he began to move in leading radical circles. Between February and August he had several meetings with perhaps the leading radical of the day, William Godwin. Two years previously, in February 1793, Godwin had published his monumental philosophical work, *Political Justice*, in which he had maintained that human beings were innately reasonable, and so could achieve perfection. But they could only do so, he argued, if all existing political and social institutions, including marriage, were destroyed. In 1794 John Thelwall, Horne Tooke, and a number of other prominent radicals, had been charged with high treason, a capital offence. Godwin had published a pamphlet, *Cursory Strictures*, in their support, and in so doing, many believed, had helped to save the accused from the gallows. For a time, Wordsworth was an ardent disciple.

Wordsworth also forged a number of long-lasting friendships while he was in London. James Losh was a committed reformer who had, like Wordsworth, witnessed the French Revolution at first hand. Basil Montagu, an illegitimate son of the fourth Earl of Sandwich, was also of a radical persuasion, and later described meeting Wordsworth as 'the most fortunate event of my life'. Recently widowed, he was struggling to earn a living as a lawyer while bringing up a young son, also called Basil. Through Montagu, Wordsworth met a liberal clergyman, Francis Wrangham, and two brothers, John Frederick and Azariah Pinney, the sons of a wealthy sugar merchant. The Pinneys, like Raisley Calvert, seem to have sensed potential greatness in Wordsworth, and they made him a generous proposal. They offered him, and Dorothy, their father's little-used house in Dorset, Racedown Lodge. It was arranged, furthermore, that they would live there rent-free, and that they would, for £50 a year, look after Montagu's son Basil. It was to prove a turning point in Wordsworth's life.

Opposite page:

A view of Keswick from Windy Brow. Wordsworth and Dorothy stayed in Keswick in 1794 and it was the home of Wordsworth's friends the Calverts.

Wordsworth Trust

 *Racedown: 1795-97*

Wordsworth arrived in Bristol in August 1795, and for the next five weeks enjoyed the city's thriving intellectual life. He met Joseph Cottle, a Unitarian publisher and bookseller, and through him two radical young poets, Robert Southey and Samuel Taylor Coleridge, then causing a stir in the city with a series of public lectures. Coleridge, in particular, impressed him; 'I wished indeed to have seen more [of him]', he wrote to Matthews, 'his talent appears to me very great.' On 22 September he was joined in Bristol by Dorothy, and four days later they and little Basil Montagu took the fifty-mile journey south to Racedown.

Racedown Lodge was a roomy Georgian house close to Lyme Regis in Dorset. It was a beautiful spot, and Wordsworth and Dorothy were soon taking daily morning walks over the neighbouring hills; 'seen from a distance', Dorothy told Jane Pollard, '[they] almost take the character of mountains, some cultivated nearly to their summits, others in their wild state covered in furze and broom. These delight me the most as they remind me of our native wilds.' It was, however, rather remote, and that first winter, wrote Dorothy, their only diversions were 'books, solitude and the fire side'. Yet, she insisted, 'I may safely say we are never dull'. They were sharing their first home together, and years later Wordsworth wrote of the strength that he drew from Dorothy's presence:

Racedown Lodge, near Lyme Regis in Dorset. Wordsworth and Dorothy lived here between 1795 and 1797. Painting by S.L. May.

Wordsworth Trust

She, in the midst of all, preserv'd me still
A Poet, made me seek beneath that name
My office upon earth, and nowhere else.

Over the winter Wordsworth made extensive alterations and additions to 'Salisbury Plain'. It remained a very bleak poem. Its purpose, he told Wrangham, was 'partly to expose the vices of the penal law and the calamities of war as they affect individuals'. Even in remote Racedown he could see the effects of Britain's war with France: 'The country people here are wretchedly poor', he wrote to Matthews, 'ignorant and overwhelmed with every vice that usually attends ignorance in that class, viz. lying and picking and stealing etc.' He also began to read voraciously. His and Dorothy's favourite part of the house was the common parlour, a civilized room which contained a piano, a sofa and armchairs. On either side of the fireplace were two large, glass-fronted mahogany bookcases, full of books on poetry, science, Italian literature, philosophy and theology.

In the new year there was a welcome visit from the ebullient Pinney brothers. During the day, Wordsworth joined them in their energetic outdoor pursuits: walking, riding, hunting and chopping wood. In the evening, everyone would gather by the fireside and talk. The Pinneys stayed at Racedown until March. 'I have since *returned* to my books', Wordsworth wrote to Matthews after their departure, but otherwise he had little else to report: 'Our present life is utterly barren of such events as merit even the short-lived chronicle of an accidental letter. We plant cabbages, and if retirement, in its full perfection, be as powerful in working transformations as one of Ovid's Gods, you may perhaps suspect that into cabbages we shall be transformed.' To Francis Wrangham he wrote asking for newspapers – 'they would be a great amusement to us in the depth of our present solitude', he told him.

But things were about to change. Azariah Pinney had left Racedown with the manuscript of the revised 'Salisbury Plain', and had given it to Joseph Cottle in Bristol. Cottle, in turn, had passed it on to Coleridge, who had known and admired Wordsworth's poetry since his days as an undergraduate at Cambridge. 'Salisbury Plain' interested him so much that he interleaved the manuscript with blank sheets of paper to allow him to write extensive notes. He was confident that the poem could

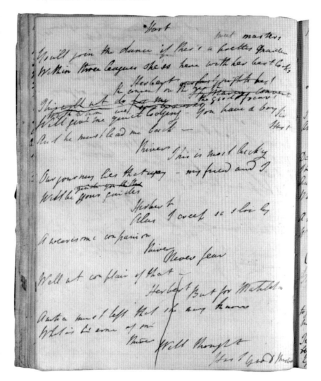

The manuscript of Wordsworth's only play, 'The Borderers', composed at Racedown in 1796-97. Efforts to get the play performed in London were unsuccessful.

Wordsworth Trust

be published, and he and Wordsworth began to correspond. By the spring, Coleridge was describing Wordsworth as 'a very dear friend', and 'the best poet of the age'. Eager to share his enthusiasm, he sent 'Salisbury Plain' to his friend Charles Lamb in London, who soon reported that he had read the poem 'not without delight'. Encouraged, no doubt, by Coleridge's admiration, Wordsworth began to write with greater energy. By the autumn he was, in Dorothy's words, 'ardent in the composition of a tragedy', *The Borderers*.

At the end of the year Mary Hutchinson came to Racedown and stayed for seven months. 'Mary Hutchinson is staying with us', wrote Dorothy in April 1797. 'She is one of the best girls in the world, and we are as happy as human beings can be.' Basil Montagu was also with them that spring. His son, little Basil, had developed wonderfully in Wordsworth's and Dorothy's care; 'He is quite metamorphosed from a shivering half-starved plant, to a lusty, blooming, fearless boy', Dorothy wrote proudly to Mrs John Marshall. 'We teach him nothing at present but what he learns from the evidence of his senses … He knows his letters, but we have not attempted any further step in the path of *book learning*. Our grand study has been to make him *happy*.' Wordsworth had also, by this time, improved remarkably. 'William is as cheerful as anybody can be', Dorothy told Mrs Marshall. 'Perhaps you may not think it, but he is the life of the whole house.'

In June Mary Hutchinson returned to the north, but only a few days after her departure Coleridge arrived. Neither Wordsworth nor Dorothy ever forgot the dramatic nature of his entrance. As he approached the house by the long, curving road, Coleridge caught sight of the Wordsworths in their orchard. Such was his eagerness to greet them that he left the road, leapt over a gate, jumped over a stream, and bounded across a field towards them. To Dorothy he made an overwhelming impression: 'His conversation teems with soul, mind and spirit', she wrote to Mary Hutchinson, 'then he is so benevolent, so good tempered and cheerful, and, like

Samuel Taylor Coleridge (left), aged twenty-three and Robert Southey (above), aged twenty-one, by Peter Vandyke.

National Portrait Gallery

William, interests himself so much about every little trifle … His eye is large and full … it speaks every emotion of his animated mind; it has more of the "poet's eye in a fine frenzy rolling" than I have ever witnessed.'

Coleridge was twenty-five, two years younger than Wordsworth, and had already crammed a remarkable amount into his life. In 1791 he had entered Cambridge University, but after a brilliant start had begun to drink heavily and fallen into debt. In 1793 he had enlisted briefly in the 18th Light Dragoons (as Silas Tomkyn Comberbache), returned to Cambridge, then left at the end of the year without taking a degree. The following year he and a friend, Robert Southey, had hatched a short-lived scheme, 'Pantisocracy', to form an ideal community in New England, and in 1795 they had lectured in Bristol to raise the necessary funds. In October that year Coleridge had married Sara Fricker, and a son, Hartley, had been born in 1796. He had also started a radical journal, *The Watchman*, and published a volume of poetry, *Poems on Various Subjects*. At the end of 1796, after abandoning pantisocracy, Coleridge had moved his family to Nether Stowey, a small village at the foot of the Quantock Hills in Somerset, some thirty miles north of Racedown.

The sympathy between the two poets was immediate, and their admiration for each other wholehearted; 'Wordsworth is a great man', Coleridge wrote simply to John Prior Estlin. They lost no time in reading their poetry to each other. 'The first thing that was read after he [Coleridge] came was William's new poem *The Ruined Cottage*', Dorothy told Mary Hutchinson, 'with which he was much delighted; and after tea he repeated to us two and a half acts of his tragedy *Osorio*; The next morning William read his tragedy *The Borderers*.'

At the end of June Coleridge returned to Nether Stowey. Four days later, the Wordsworths followed after him. They did not know it, but they would never return to Racedown. The house, however, never lost its hold over their affections. 'Racedown was the first home I had', Dorothy later wrote. 'I think it is the place dearest to my recollections upon the whole surface of the islands.'

≈ *Alfoxden: 1797-98*

Coleridge's home at Nether Stowey was a tiny, run-down cottage on the western edge of the village. There, with his wife Sara and baby son Hartley, he lived a deliberately simple life: he read, wrote, and kept pigs. His closest friend in the village was Thomas Poole, the owner of the local tannery. Poole was well known in Bristol for his democratic opinions, and immediately impressed Wordsworth as a kind and considerate employer. 'During my residence at Alfoxden', Wordsworth said many years later, 'I used to see much of him [Poole] and had frequent occasions to admire the conduct of his daily life, especially his conduct to his labourers and poor neighbours … he felt for all men as his brothers.'

Less than a week after the Wordsworths' arrival, the already crammed cottage received another visitor, Charles Lamb. Lamb had known Coleridge since their days together at Christ's Hospital school in London, and several of his verses had been published in Coleridge's 1796 *Poems*. Though by nature a witty and amiable man, Lamb was subdued during his week at Nether Stowey; he was still in shock from the tragedy that had befallen him the previous autumn – his sister Mary, in a fit of madness, had fatally stabbed their mother. But he benefitted greatly from the warm mood of the household, and every day would join the Wordsworths in their explorations of the surrounding countryside. 'There is everything here', Dorothy enthused to Mary Hutchinson, 'sea, woods wild as fancy ever painted, brooks clear and pebbly as in Cumberland, villages so romantic … Walks extend for miles over the hilltops; the great beauty of which is their wild simplicity.'

Wanting to be close to Coleridge, Wordsworth and Dorothy set about looking for nearby accommodation. Fortunately, they did not have to look for long. On one of their walks they came across Alfoxden House, a large property four miles from Nether Stowey. It was ideal: fully furnished, close to the sea, and within easy walking distance from Coleridge. With Poole's help they obtained a one year lease, and on 16 July moved in. Dorothy described their new home to Mary Hutchinson:

Here we are in a large mansion, in a large park, with seventy head of deer around us … From the end of the house we have a view of the sea, over a woody meadow-country; and exactly opposite the window where I now sit is an immense wood, whose round top from this point has exactly the appearance of a mighty dome … wherever we turn we have woods, smooth downs, and valleys with small brooks running down them through green meadows, hardly ever intersected with hedgerows, but scattered over with trees.

To celebrate their arrival, Wordsworth and Dorothy held a large dinner party. There were fourteen guests, including the writer and orator John Thelwall, who was staying with the Coleridges at Nether Stowey. Thelwall was a notorious radical, and his presence among a group of people who took strange moonlit walks and who had no obvious employment aroused local suspicions. The country was living in fear of a French invasion, and people were on the lookout for spies. Accordingly, a Home Office agent, Mr Walsh, was dispatched to investigate. Walsh questioned servants

and neighbours, and concluded that though they were not French spies, the inhabitants of Alfoxden House were nevertheless 'a mischievous gang of disaffected Englishmen', and 'a Sett of violent Democrats'.

In truth, agitation was the last thing on anyone's mind. Thelwall's spirit had been broken by constant, often violent resistance to his activities. He had come to the south west of England in search of peace; the attraction of the area, he said, was that it enabled him to forget 'all the jarrings and conflicts of the wide world'. Coleridge later recalled one telling moment: 'We were once sitting in a beautiful recess in the Quantocks, when I said to him, "Citizen John, this is a fine place to talk treason in!" – "Nay! Citizen Samuel," replied he, "it is rather a place to make a man forget that there is any necessity for treason!"' Thelwall went on to settle on a farm in neighbouring Wales, and remembered his time in Somerset with fondness.

The Wordsworths had impressed him; in a poem written after his departure he described Wordsworth finely as 'Alfoxden's musing tenant', and Dorothy as 'the maid / Of ardent eye, who, with fraternal love, / Sweetens his solitude'.

Wordsworth and Coleridge were also losing interest in direct political activity. Increasingly, their delight was in rural retirement, and in each other's company. The journal that Dorothy kept at Alfoxden shows that she, Wordsworth and Coleridge were in almost daily contact, and wonderfully alive to the subtle beauties of the landscape:

> *...walked with Coleridge nearly to Stowey after dinner. A very clear afternoon. We lay sidelong upon the turf, and gazed on the landscape till it melted into more than natural loveliness. The sea very uniform, of a pale greyish blue, only one distant bay, bright and blue as a sky; had there been a vessel sailing up it, a perfect image of delight.*

Their great passion was poetry, and in November 1797 both poets embarked upon an extraordinary period of creativity. That month Coleridge composed 'Kubla Khan', the visionary poem which, he later claimed, was written under the influence of opium, a drug commonly taken as painkiller. Then, on a walking tour along the coast, Wordsworth and Coleridge came up with the idea for 'The Rime of the Ancient Mariner'. It began as a collaboration, but soon Coleridge was writing alone. He worked hard over the winter, and in March 1798 read the completed poem to the Wordsworths. By this time, Wordsworth had himself begun to write in earnest. He had returned to a poem from his Racedown days, 'The Ruined Cottage', which told the story of Margaret, and her slow, painful decline after her husband leaves her to enlist in the army. He now developed this 'tale of silent suffering' into one of consolation, finding in Margaret's persistent hope an enduring strength. Her ruined cottage became a place of tranquillity, living evidence of

A group of portraits made between 1796 and 1798 by Robert Hancock, and commissioned by Wordsworth's Bristol publisher, Joseph Cottle. From left to right: Wordsworth, Coleridge, Lamb and Southey.

Wordsworth Trust

43

William Wordsworth

That secret spring of humanity
Which, mid the calm oblivious tendencies
Of Nature, mid her plants, her weeds and flowers,
And silent overgrowings, still survived.

As Wordsworth grew more confident, Coleridge remained unstinting in his admiration and encouragement: 'I have known him [Wordsworth] a year and some months', he wrote to his friend Estlin, 'and my admiration, I might say my awe, of his intellectual powers has increased even to this hour, and (what is of more importance) he is a tried good man.' Wordsworth's destiny, as far as Coleridge was concerned, was to be the greatest philosophical poet of the age, and that spring he almost certainly inspired the grand scheme that was to haunt Wordsworth for the rest of his life. In the first week of March Wordsworth told his friend James Tobin that he was busy with a poem 'in which I continue to convey most of the knowledge of which I am possessed ... I know not anything which will not come within the scope of my plan.' Five days later he told James Losh: 'I have written 1300 lines of a poem which I hope to make of considerable utility. Its title will be *The Recluse; or Views of Nature, Man and Society.'* For the moment, however, these thirteen hundred lines, which may be a reference to 'The Ruined Cottage', were as far as Wordsworth was to get with 'The Recluse'. Instead, he started to write verse of a very different kind.

The poetry that Wordsworth now turned to was revolutionary. Its subject was the lives and feelings of people who up till then had not been considered at all poetic: the very poor, the very young, the deranged; tinkers, shepherds and huntsmen. And it used the simplest, most unadorned language. One poem followed another in a period of astonishing invention: 'Goody Blake and Harry Gill', 'The Idiot Boy', 'We are Seven', 'The Thorn', 'Peter Bell', 'Simon Lee', 'The Mad Mother', all date from this period. 'His faculties seem to expand every day', Dorothy told Mary Hutchinson. 'He composes with much more facility than he did, as to the *mechanism* of poetry, and his ideas flower faster than he can express them.' Years later, in *The Prelude*, Wordsworth himself recalled this magical spring, 'wherein we first / Together wandered in wild poesy'. He was writing 'The Idiot Boy' and 'The Thorn', Coleridge 'The Rime of the Ancient Mariner' and 'Christabel':

> *That summer when on Quantock's grassy hills*
> *Far ranging, and among the sylvan coombs,*
> *Thou in delicious words, with happy heart,*
> *Didst speak the vision of that ancient man,*
> *The bright-eyed Mariner, and rueful woes*
> *Didst utter of the Lady Christabel;*
> *And I, associate in such labour, walked*
> *Murmuring of him, who – joyous hap – was found,*
> *After the perils of his moonlight ride,*
> *Near the loud waterfall, or her who sate*
> *In misery near the miserable thorn …*

In May, the young writer William Hazlitt came to Nether Stowey. In a magnificent essay written over twenty years later, *On My First Acquaintance with Poets*, he vividly recalled his introduction both to Wordsworth's poetry – 'the sense of a new style and a new spirit in poetry came over me' – and to Wordsworth himself. It is one of the finest of all descriptions of the poet:

> *I think I see him now. He answered in some degree to his friend's description*
> *of him, but was more gaunt and Don Quixote-like. He was quaintly dressed*
> *(according to the costume of that unconstrained period) in a brown fustian*
> *jacket and striped pantaloons. There was something of a roll, a lounge in his*
> *gait, not unlike his own Peter Bell. There was a severe, worn pressure of*

thought about his temples, a fire in his eye (as if he saw something in objects more than outward appearance) an intense, high narrow forehead, a Roman nose, cheeks furrowed by strong purpose and feeling, and a convulsive inclination to laughter about the mouth, a good deal at variance with the solemn, stately expression of the rest of his features ... He sat down and talked very naturally and freely, with a mixture of clear, gushing accents in his voice, a deep guttural intonation, a strong tincture of northern burr, like the crust on wine. He instantly began to make havoc of the half of Cheshire cheese on the table ...

By this time the Wordsworths' tenancy of Alfoxden was running out. There was, however, a plan that would keep everyone together: Wordsworth, Dorothy and Coleridge would all go to Germany, where, Wordsworth told Losh, 'we purpose to pass the two ensuing years in order to acquire the German language, and to furnish ourselves with a tolerable stock of information in natural science. Our plan is to settle, if possible, in a village near a university, in a pleasant, and, if we can, a mountainous, country.'

The weeks leading up to the departure for Germany were eventful. At the end of June Wordsworth and Dorothy vacated Alfoxden and moved to Bristol. After the calm of the countryside, the noise of the city was almost too much for Dorothy: 'I am writing in a front room, in one of the most busy streets of Bristol', she told Mary Hutchinson. 'You can scarcely conceive how the jarring contrast between the sounds which are now for ever ringing in my ears and the sweet sounds of Alfoxden makes me long for the country again. After three years residence in retirement a city in feeling, sound and prospect is hateful.' On 10 July she and Wordsworth went on a walking tour of the Wye Valley. It was a welcome break from the city, and, for Wordsworth, a reminder of a previous summer, five years before, when he had walked the same paths along the Wye, alone and in very different circumstances. Then he had been restless and anxious. Now, in Dorothy's company, he was inspired to write his greatest poem to date. 'Lines written a few miles above Tintern Abbey' is an expression of Wordsworth's new-found faith in nature, in human passions, and the power of the imagination. It is both a celebration of the last year in Somerset, and its magnificent conclusion:

> *I have felt*
>
> *A presence that disturbs me with the joy*
> *Of elevated thoughts; a sense sublime*
> *Of something far more deeply interfused,*
> *Whose dwelling is the light of setting suns,*
> *And the round ocean, and the living air,*
> *And the blue sky, and in the mind of man,*
> *A motion and a spirit, that impels*
> *All thinking things, all objects of all thought,*
> *And rolls through all things. Therefore am I still*
> *A lover of the meadows and the woods,*
> *And mountains; and of all that we behold*
> *From this green earth; of all the mighty world*
> *Of eye and ear, both what they half-create,*
> *And what perceive; well pleased to recognize*
> *In nature and the language of the sense,*
> *The anchor of my purest thoughts, the nurse,*
> *The guide, the guardian of my heart, and soul*
> *Of all my moral being.*

After four days in the Wye valley, Wordsworth and Dorothy returned to Bristol. They were just in time to include 'Tintern Abbey' in the volume that Wordsworth was now publishing in collaboration with Coleridge, *Lyrical Ballads and other Poems*. Now seen as one of the key publications of the Romantic period, at the time it was chiefly an attempt to raise funds for the German trip. Coleridge contributed 'The Rime of the Ancient Mariner', which opened the volume, and four other pieces. The rest of the book consisted largely of poems written by Wordsworth at Alfoxden. 'Tintern Abbey' concluded the volume. *Lyrical Ballads* was, at Coleridge's insistence, published anonymously; 'Wordsworth's name is nothing', he told Joseph Cottle, the publisher, 'to a large number of people mine *stinks*.' In a prefatory 'Advertisement' Wordsworth described the poems as 'experiments', written 'chiefly with a view to ascertain how far the language of conversation in the middle and lower classes of society is adapted to the purposes of poetic pleasure'.

Lyrical Ballads was printed in or around the first week of September. Later that month Wordsworth, Dorothy and Coleridge, together with John Chester, a friend of Coleridge's from Nether Stowey, set sail from Yarmouth.

Germany and the North East: 1798-99

The passage across the North Sea to Germany took two days, and both Wordsworth and Dorothy proved to be bad sailors. 'Wordsworth shockingly ill, his Sister worst of all – vomiting, & groaning, unspeakably!' wrote Coleridge in a letter to his wife, adding with some pride that he, by contrast, was 'neither sick nor giddy but gay as a lark'. On 18 September the party reached the mouth of the river Elbe, and the following day arrived at Hamburg.

Coleridge was enthralled by the unfamiliar sights and sounds of the city. Dorothy, on the other hand, was disgusted by Hamburg's 'dirty, ill-paved stinking streets', and by the easy dishonesty of its inhabitants; 'I have constantly observed a disposition to cheat, and take advantage of our ignorance', she wrote sharply in her journal. Wordsworth summed up his feelings to Thomas Poole: 'It is a *sad* place, in this epithet you have the soul and essence of all the information which I have been able to gather.' The highlight of their stay was a visit to Friedrich Klopstock, the elderly poet considered by Coleridge to be 'the venerable father of German poetry'. Wordsworth exchanged views with him as best he could in French, but found him to be disappointingly ignorant of English poetry, and, in person, hardly the image of a poet: his legs were badly swollen, and his face, Wordsworth noted, did not bear 'the marks either of sublimity or enthusiasm'.

After two weeks in Hamburg the Wordsworths and Coleridge separated. Coleridge was eager to learn German and study the great German philosophers, and on 30 September he left for the fashionable town of Ratzeburgh some thirty miles to the east. Wordsworth and Dorothy, lacking Coleridge's clarity of purpose and financially much more constrained, remained in Hamburg and looked around for somewhere to pass the winter. They decided on Goslar, a town two hundred miles to the south, at the foot of the Hartz Mountains in Lower Saxony. It seemed a good choice, for Goslar boasted a distinguished history, and had the great advantage of

The 'venerable father of German poetry', Friedrich Klopstock, whom Wordsworth and Coleridge met in Hamburg in 1798. Engraving after a portrait by Tuel, 1801.

Wordsworth Trust

being cheap, but when they arrived there on 6 October the Wordsworths were disappointed. Badly damaged over the years by fire and war, Goslar turned out to be no more than a dull provincial town – 'once the residence of Kings, now the residence of Grocers and Linen-drapers' wrote Wordsworth to Thomas Poole.

Wordsworth and Dorothy stayed in Goslar for five lonely months. The worst winter of the century allowed them only the briefest of daily walks, and so most of their time was spent in the cheap lodgings they had taken with a draper's widow. Even indoors they had to wear greatcoats to protect themselves from the penetrating cold. Nor did Wordsworth learn much German, as he depended for conversation on a neighbour who was both toothless and deaf; 'with bad German, bad English, bad French, bad hearing, and bad utterance', Wordsworth wrote to Josiah Wedgwood, 'you will imagine that we have had very pretty dialogues'. Goslar society, such as it was, ignored them, and Coleridge, who was enjoying a productive and sociable life in Ratzeburg, guessed why: 'His [Wordsworth] taking his sister with him was a

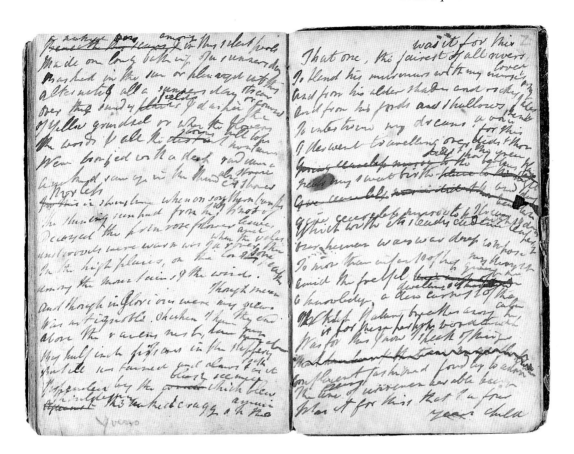

wrong step', he wrote to his wife. 'It is next to impossible for any but married women or in the suit of married women to be introduced to any company in Germany. Sister [here] is considered as only a name for Mistress. – Still however *male* acquaintance he might have had – & had I been at Goslar, I *would* have had them – but W., God love him! Seems to have lost his spirits & almost his inclination for it.'

Isolated, and intensely homesick, Wordsworth withdrew into himself. His thoughts turned to the Lake District, and to his earliest childhood memories: the music of the River Derwent as it flowed along the bottom of his garden in Cockermouth; skating on Esthwaite Water; and how, one moonlit night, he had stolen a shepherd's boat and rowed out on to Ullswater. Inspired by the conviction that it was in these early experiences that he would find the foundations for his creative adult life, Wordsworth began to shape his thoughts into verse, and so began, in its earliest form, his great autobiographical poem, *The Prelude*. It was an intense, exhausting process: 'I should have written five times as much as I have done',

An early manuscript of Wordsworth's greatest work, The Prelude, *begun at Goslar in the winter of 1798-99. By the end of 1799 Wordsworth had completed a two-part version of the poem.*

Wordsworth Trust

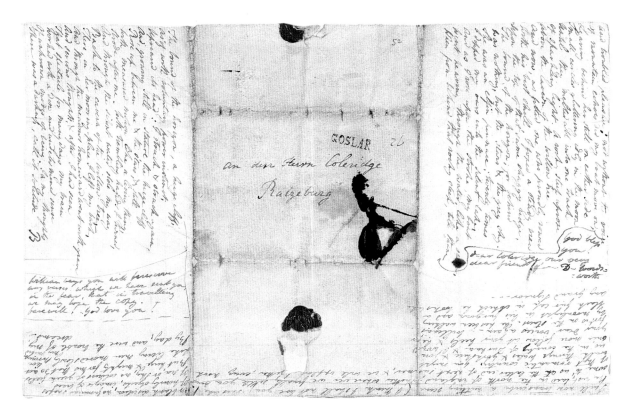

Wordsworth wrote to Coleridge in February 1799, 'but that I am prevented by an uneasiness at my stomach and side, with a dull pain about my heart … I am absolutely consumed by thinking and feeling.'

In February the winter began to abate, and Wordsworth and Dorothy were anxious to depart. They left Goslar at the end of the month, and spent the next few weeks rambling through the Hartz Mountains. In April they arrived at the ancient university town of Göttingen, where Coleridge was now living. They had missed each other keenly, and it was an emotional reunion, but Coleridge noticed that Wordsworth was full of 'impatience to return to their native country'. Within a week Wordsworth and Dorothy were back in Hamburg, and by the end of April they had reached England, after nearly eight months abroad.

Almost immediately they proceeded north to Sockburn-on-Tees in County Durham, the home of Mary Hutchinson and her family. There, in familiar surroundings once more, Wordsworth took stock. In May he wrote to his brother Richard requesting information about his precarious financial position. Richard's news was bad. Wordsworth had invested most of his legacy from Raisely Calvert in loans to a friend of Basil Montagu's, Charles Douglas, and Montagu himself. Both had defaulted on their payments, and he therefore found himself unable to repay an outstanding loan from Coleridge's patron, the pottery maker Josiah Wedgwood, which had largely sustained him in Germany. Then he learned from Joseph Cottle that sales of *Lyrical Ballads* had been disappointing. To his great chagrin he discovered that Robert Southey had written a largely unfavourable notice of the volume in the *Critical Review* – 'He knew that money was of importance to me', he complained to Cottle. 'If he could not conscientiously have spoken differently of the volume, he ought to have declined the task of reviewing it.'

Then there was the question of where he and Dorothy were to live. This had been troubling them for some time. 'Wordsworth is divided in his mind', Coleridge had written to Poole back in January, 'unquietly divided, between the neighbourhood of Stowey & the N. of England. He cannot think of settling at a distance from *me*, & I have told him that I *cannot* leave the vicinity of Stowey.' But it wasn't long before Coleridge was with them once more, if only as a visitor. In July he returned from

On the Greta
by John Sell Cotman,
1806. Wordsworth and
Coleridge passed
through Greta Bridge
on their way to the
Lake District in 1799.

Norfolk Museums Service
(Norwich Castle Museum)

Germany, and in October, together with Joseph Cottle, he arrived at Sockburn. Five days after his arrival, he, Cottle and Wordsworth set out for a walking tour of the Lake District.

The tour was to last just under three weeks. Soon after their departure, at Greta Bridge, Cottle broke off and returned to London. But further on, at Temple Sowerby near the north east border of the Lake District, Wordsworth and Coleridge were joined by Wordsworth's sailor brother John, then enjoying a rare break from the sea. Together they entered the Lake District from the north, walking south through Kentmere to Troutbeck and Hawkshead. From there they proceeded north through the central fells to Ambleside and Grasmere. At Grisedale John Wordsworth left them, while Wordsworth and Coleridge continued north to Keswick. The second part of their journey took them to the wilder lakes in the west: Buttermere, Ennerdale and Wastwater. Finally, they looped back to the north east, ending up at Pooley Bridge on the northern shore of Ullswater. Here they visited the anti-Slave Trade campaigner, Thomas Clarkson, and his wife Catherine, who was considerably impressed by Wordsworth: 'Wordsworth has a fine commanding figure', she wrote, 'is rather handsome & looks as if he was born to be a great Prince or a great General. He seems very fond of C[oleridge] laughing at all his jokes & taking all opportunities of showing him off & to crown all he has the manners of a gentleman.'

This tour was to have a momentous effect on both poets. For Coleridge, it was an overwhelming introduction to a new kind of landscape – 'how deeply I have been impressed by a world of scenery absolutely new to me', he wrote afterwards to Dorothy. 'It was to me a vision of a fair Country.' The combined attractions of Lake District scenery and the Wordsworths' company was soon to lure him north again. For Wordsworth, it was to lead to a return to his native soil. At Grasmere he had seen a small cottage available for rent, and after separating from Coleridge at Pooley Bridge he returned there to arrange a lease. From then on events moved quickly. By the time Wordsworth had arrived back at Sockburn on 26 November all the necessary arrangements to take the cottage had been made, and on 17 December he and Dorothy left Sockburn for Grasmere. After a dramatic winter journey through the Yorkshire Dales they reached Kendal, where they bought furniture. On the evening of 20 December they arrived at their new home in Grasmere.

Dove Cottage: 1799-1801

In October 1769 the poet Thomas Gray had passed through Grasmere, and described the valley in his journal: 'Not a single red tile, no flaring gentleman's house, or garden walls, break in upon the repose of this little unsuspected paradise; but all is peace, rusticity, and happy poverty, in its neatest, most becoming attire.' Some years later, Wordsworth had, as a schoolboy, walked to Grasmere from Hawkshead. He too had thought it a paradise:

> *What happy fortune were it here to live!*
> *And if a thought of dying, if a thought*
> *Of mortal separation could come in*
> *With paradise before me, here to die.*

Now he was fulfilling this childhood dream. 'Embrace me, then, ye Hills, and close me in' he wrote in 'Home at Grasmere', a poem he began soon after his arrival. He had come to 'this sublime retirement' to write poetry. Here he could dedicate himself to the great task of writing 'The Recluse':

> *Yet in this peaceful Vale we will not spend*
> *Unheard-of days, though loving peaceful thoughts;*
> *A Voice shall speak, and what will be the theme?*
> *On Man, on Nature, and on human Life,*
> *Thinking in solitude, from time to time*
> *I feel sweet passions traversing my Soul*
> *Like Music; unto these, where'er I may,*
> *I would give utterance in numerous verse.*
> *Of truth, of grandeur, beauty, love, and hope—*
> *Hope for this earth and hope beyond the grave;*
> *Of virtue and of intellectual power;*
> *Of blessed consolations in distress;*
> *Of joy in widest commonalty spread;*

Of the individual mind that keeps its own
Inviolate retirement, and consists
With being limitless, the one great Life,
I sing: fit audience let me find, though few!

'A little unsuspected paradise': Grasmere from the Rydal Road by Francis Towne, c.1787.

Birmingham Museum and Art Gallery

Wordsworth's and Dorothy's new home, now known as Dove Cottage, was a small lakeland dwelling dating from the early seventeenth century, one of the handful of cottages and farm buildings that made up Town End, a hamlet just outside Grasmere village itself. They arrived in the evening to find it dark and unfurnished: there were beds in the rooms upstairs, and a dying fire in the gloomy parlour, but otherwise the house was empty. Still, they were undismayed; 'We were young and healthy and had obtained an object long desired', Dorothy later recalled. 'We had returned to our native mountains, there to live.'

Four days after their arrival, on Christmas Eve, Wordsworth wrote a long letter to Coleridge. Both he and Dorothy, he said, had caught troublesome colds, and Dorothy was 'racked with the tooth-ache', but he was confident that they could make

the house into a comfortable dwelling. From the highest point of the steeply sloping garden, 'our little domestic slip of mountain', they could see two thirds of the vale: the lake, the church, and the surrounding fells. Here they hoped to build a summer house. The front of the cottage looked on to the main road, and they planned to

This sihouette miniature is the only known likeness of Dorothy Wordsworth as a young woman. It was made by an unknown artist in about 1806, while she was living at Dove Cottage.

Wordsworth Trust

create a small front garden, 'for the sake of a few flowers, and because it will make it more our own'. Their neighbours, he said, 'we have uniformly found kind-hearted frank and manly'. There was a keen frost, and the next day he meant to go skating on the neighbouring lake of Rydal.

The life Wordsworth and Dorothy led at Dove Cottage was frugal and committed. It was also, from the very beginning, a life they shared with others. Previously, Wordsworth had travelled the country in order to be with friends. Now that he was settled in Grasmere, these friends came to him. For the next eight years, Dove Cottage was hardly ever without visitors. The first to arrive was his brother John. He came at the end of January 1800, and stayed until the end of September. John was a reticent man (his father had once described him as 'Ibex, the shyest of all the beasts'), but deeply sensitive to all around him. To Wordsworth he was a 'silent Poet' who possessed 'a watchful heart' and 'an eye practised like a blind man's touch'. John fitted easily into their lives; he had, Dorothy wrote, 'a perfect sympathy with all our pleasures'.

Mary Hutchinson came in late February, and stayed for six weeks. Immediately after her departure, Coleridge arrived. He did not, on this occasion, stay long, returning to Nether Stowey the following month, but in June he was back again, this time to stay. He, Sara and Hartley went to live at Greta Hall in Keswick, twelve miles to the north. The Alfoxden group was together again, and, undeterred by the twelve-mile walk between Grasmere and Keswick, Wordsworth and Coleridge were continual visitors to each other's homes over the coming months. Others were drawn to Grasmere that first year: Thomas and Catherine Clarkson became close friends; James Losh travelled up from the south, and Wordsworth's Cambridge friend Robert Jones from Wales; at the end of the year, they were joined by Mary Hutchinson's sister Sara.

In May 1800 Dorothy began a journal, and continued it for the next two and a half years. As one reads it now, the Wordsworths' day-to-day existence at Dove Cottage comes to life. Dorothy records everything, from the reading and writing of poetry to the smallest domestic details. She records her and Wordsworth's exchanges with the local inhabitants and their chance meetings with travellers, vagrants and solitaries on the road. She records the visitors to the cottage, and their daily activities of walking, gardening, fishing and boating. Private and intimate, intended only for herself and her brother, Dorothy's journal captures the intense emotions of the first years at Dove Cottage:

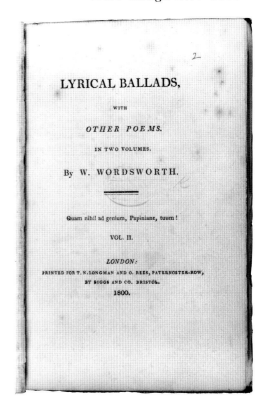

Sunday 20th [June 1802]. After tea we walked upon our own path for a long time. We talked sweetly together about the disposal of our riches. We lay upon the sloping Turf. Earth & sky were so lovely that they melted our very hearts. The sky to the north was of a chastened yet rich yellow fading into pale blue & streaked & scattered over with steady islands of purple melting away into shades of pink. It made my heart almost feel like a vision to me.

The journal also reveals Dorothy's skill as a descriptive writer. At Nether Stowey, Coleridge had remarked upon her talent for observation: 'Her eye watchful in minutest observation of nature; and her taste a perfect electrometer. It bends, protrudes, and draws in, at subtlest beauties and most recondite faults.'

On 29 August 1800 Dorothy noted in her journal:

At 11 o'clock Coleridge came when I was walking in the still, clear moonshine in the garden—he came over Helvellyn—Wm was gone to bed & John also, worn out with his ride round Coniston. We sate & chatted till ¹/2 past three W in his dressing gown. Coleridge read us part of Christabel. Talked much about the mountains &c &c ...

'Christabel' was Coleridge's latest poem, a supernatural tale of witchery and romance. Once finished, it was to be included in the volume he and Wordsworth were now planning, a second edition of *Lyrical Ballads*. The book appeared at the beginning of the following year, in two volumes. The first volume contained,

The second, enlarged edition of Lyrical Ballads *was published in two volumes at the beginning of 1800. All but one of the new poems were Wordsworth's, and the title page identified him as the sole author of the work.*

The British Library, C58.c.12

reordered and somewhat revised, the poems from the first edition. The second volume was largely comprised of new poems written by Wordsworth during his first year at Dove Cottage: 'Hart-Leap Well', 'The Waterfall and the Eglantine', 'Rural Architecture', 'Poems on the Naming of Places', 'The Brothers' and 'Michael'. The last two are among Wordsworth's finest works, and were concerned with the Lake District 'statesmen', owners of small estates who lived an independent life among the hills. Wordsworth described his intentions in writing 'Michael' to Thomas Poole: 'I have attempted to give a picture of a man, of strong mind and lively sensibility, agitated by two of the most powerful affections of the human heart; the parental affection, and the love of property, *landed* property, including the feelings of inheritance, home, and personal and family independence.' In presenting a copy of

A draft of 'Michael', composed at Dove Cottage, published in the second edition of Lyrical Ballads, *and written, Wordsworth told Charles James Fox, to show that 'men who do not wear fine cloaths can feel deeply'.*

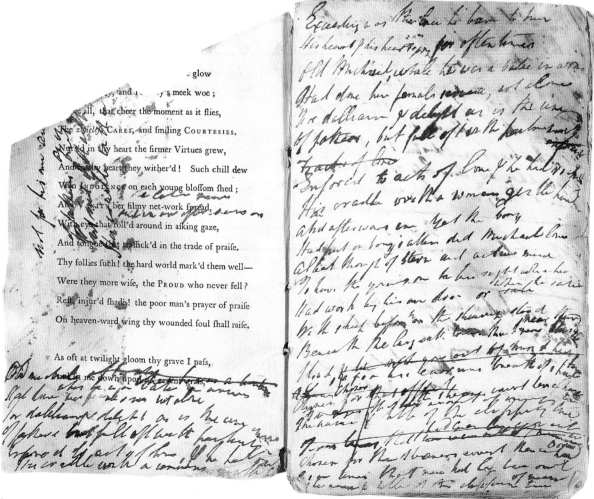

Lyrical Ballads to the politician Charles James Fox, he went further. 'Michael' and 'The Brothers', he told Fox, 'were written with a view to shew that men who do not wear fine cloaths can feel deeply.'

The second edition of *Lyrical Ballads* contained a lengthy preface. Here Wordsworth first articulated the theories of poetry that he and Coleridge had been developing since the days in Somerset. The poems of *Lyrical Ballads* were written, he explained, 'to make the incidents of common life interesting by tracing in them, truly though not ostentatiously, the primary laws of our nature: chiefly as far as regards the manner in which we associate ideas in a state of excitement'. Poetry he memorably defined as 'the spontaneous overflow of powerful feelings: it takes its origin from emotion recollected in tranquillity'.

It was Coleridge who had urged Wordsworth to write the preface – Wordsworth himself later said that he 'never cared a straw about the theory'. Indeed, it was Coleridge who had provided most of the energy behind the whole publication. But his own poetic contribution was now well below Wordsworth's, and the new title page made this quite clear. While the first edition of *Lyrical Ballads* had been published anonymously, the second edition said categorically: *Lyrical Ballads, with other poems. In Two Volumes. By William Wordsworth*. Wordsworth had assumed sole ownership. 'Christabel', the poem that was to have been Coleridge's major contribution, remained unfinished, and had not, at Wordsworth's insistence, been included. Coleridge tried to explain its ommission to a friend, the chemist Humphry Davy: 'the poem was in direct opposition to the very purpose for which the *Lyrical Ballads* were published', he wrote, 'viz—an experiment to see how far those passions, which alone give any value to extraordinary incidents, were capable of interesting, in and for themselves, in the incidents of common life.' But its exclusion must nevertheless have been a great disappointment. At Alfoxden Wordsworth and Coleridge had been equal partners. Now, full of self-doubt, Coleridge increasingly felt that Wordsworth's achievements were superior to his own: 'as to our literary occupations they are still more distant than our residences', he wrote in December. 'He is a great, a true Poet – I am only a kind of Metaphysician.'

Dove Cottage: 1801-5

The second year at Dove Cottage was quieter than the first. There is a gap in Dorothy's journal from December 1800 to October 1801, and Wordsworth wrote little. In the spring, John Wordsworth, now captain of the merchant ship the *Earl of Abergavenny*, departed for a lengthy voyage. Coleridge was ill for much of the year, and in November left the Lake District to winter in the south.

At the beginning of 1802 Wordsworth and Mary Hutchinson became engaged. Friends, when they heard the news, were unsurprised. Mary had been a friend of the family since childhood, and during her long stay at Racedown she and Wordsworth had become deeply attached. She had also become part of life at Dove Cottage. On a stone midway between Grasmere and Keswick, the so-called 'Rock of Names', Wordsworth and his closest friends had carved their initials; Mary's appeared alongside those of Wordsworth, Dorothy, Coleridge, John Wordsworth and Sara Hutchinson.

The new year also brought fresh composition. Wordsworth was again revising 'The Ruined Cottage', now known as 'The Pedlar'. He was also writing new poetry: 'Alice Fell', 'Beggars' and 'To H.C., Six Years Old', a poem to Hartley Coleridge. At the end of March, over breakfast, he began one of his greatest poems, 'Ode. Intimations of Immortality from Recollections of Early Childhood', an event recorded by Dorothy in her Journal: 'A divine morning—at Breakfast Wm wrote part of an ode—Mr Olliff sent the Dung & Wm went to work in the garden we sate all day in the Orchard.' Then in May he started another major poem, known amongst family and friends as 'The Leech Gatherer', but later published as 'Resolution and Independence'. In October 1800 he and Dorothy had encountered an old man by the road who, they were dismayed to discover, had lost nine of his ten children. His trade, Dorothy had written in her journal, 'was to gather leeches but now leeches were scarce & he had not strength for it – he lived by begging & was making his way to Carlisle where he should buy a few godly books to sell'. Now, almost two years later, Wordsworth returned to this memorable encounter, finding in it a supreme example of human fortitude and dignity in the face of adversity:

The Old Man still stood talking by my side;

But now his voice to me was like a stream

Scarce heard; nor word from word could I divide;

And the whole Body of the man did seem

Like one whom I had met with in a dream;

Or like a Man from some far region sent;

To give me human strength, and strong admonishment.

That summer, the Peace of Amiens brought a truce between England and France. It was an unexpected opportunity for Wordsworth to see Annette Vallon and, for the first time, his daughter Caroline, and in July he and Dorothy left Dove Cottage for France. At the beginning of August they arrived in Calais, where they had arranged to meet Annette and Caroline. In the evenings they would all walk along the shore and talk, but here Dorothy's journal falls silent, and we know nothing of what passed between them. We do know, however, that Wordsworth and Dorothy stayed in Calais for a month, which suggests that Wordsworth was keen to maintain his friendship with the woman so central to his early life, and to make friends with his daughter.

Wordsworth and Dorothy arrived back in England in September, and headed straight for the Hutchinsons' home in the north east. On 4 October, shortly after 8 o'clock in the morning, Wordsworth and Mary Hutchinson were married. Immediately after the wedding breakfast, Wordsworth, Mary and Dorothy began the journey back to Dove Cottage. Dorothy, overcome by many conflicting emotions, had been unable to attend the ceremony. She and her brother had shared a house together for seven intense years; now, she knew, that period of their lives was ending. There is a revealing passage in her journal, written on the morning of the wedding, and later heavily deleted, possibly by Dorothy herself:

At a little after 8 o clock I saw them go down the avenue towards the church. William had parted from me up stairs. I gave him the wedding ring—with how deep a blessing! I took it from my forefinger where I had worn it the whole of the night before – he slipped it again onto my finger and blessed me fervently.

But she loved Mary as a sister, and had no fears for the union. It was, indeed, to be an exceptionally successful marriage. Mary's calm, self-effacing presence, and the domestic tranquillity that came with it, sustained Wordsworth for the rest of his life. 'It does a man's heart good, I will not say, to know such a family', commented Coleridge, 'but even – to know that there is such a Family … [Wordsworth's] is the happiest Family, I ever saw.'

Coleridge's own life, by contrast, was now in serious decline. Plagued by ill health, he had turned to opium for relief, and was now seriously addicted to the drug. His marriage was in pieces, and he had developed a hopeless, obsessive love for Mary Hutchinson's sister Sara. In April he had written his 'Letter to Sara Hutchinson', in which he had brooded upon his unhappiness and the decline of his creative powers.

Later in the month he had read the poem to the Wordsworths: 'Coleridge came to us and repeated the verses he wrote to Sara', Dorothy had written in her journal. 'I was affected with them & was on the whole, not being well, in miserable spirits.' With heavy irony, a revised version of the poem, 'Dejection: An Ode', appeared in the *Morning Post* on Wordsworth's wedding day.

In June 1803 William and Mary Wordsworth's first child, John, was born. Two months later Wordsworth, Coleridge and Dorothy set off for a tour of Scotland. But as an attempt to reunite the old Alfoxden group it failed. Signs of strain soon began to show, and after only two weeks, the Wordsworths and Coleridge separated. Coleridge, ill himself, apparently found Wordsworth 'hypochondriacal ... silent and self-centered'. In October, he was complaining to Thomas Poole that Wordsworth was 'more and more benetted in hypochondriacal fancies, living wholly among *devotees* – having even the minutest thing, almost his very eating and drinking, done for him by his sister, or wife ...'.

Wordsworth and Dorothy continued alone. They reached as far north as Glencoe and Killiecrankie in the Scottish Highlands, then returned through the Trossachs, Linlithgow, Edinburgh and Melrose, arriving back at Grasmere on 25 September. Dorothy recalled their six-week tour in her *Recollections of a Tour made in Scotland*, while a number of Wordsworth's best-known poems derive from this trip, including 'Stepping Westward' and 'The Solitary Reaper'.

In Edinburgh Wordsworth had been introduced to Walter Scott. Scott's passion for the Border country was equal to Wordsworth's for the Lake District, and the two writers struck up an immediate friendship. 'My sister and I often talk of the happy days which we passed in your Company', Wordsworth wrote to Scott from Grasmere, '... such things do not occur often in life. If we live, we shall meet again that is my consolation when I think of these things.'

In 1805 Scott came to Keswick, and Wordsworth took him and Humphry Davy up Helvellyn, one of the Lake District's highest peaks. During the ascent, Wordsworth said afterwards, the party had been 'beguiled by Scott's telling stories and amusing anecdote as was his custom'. Scott, for his part, described Wordsworth to the poet Anna Seward as 'such a character as only exists in romance, virtuous, simple, and unaffectedly restricting every want and wish to the bounds of a very

narrow income in order to enjoy the literary and poetical leisure which his happiness consists in'.

Wordsworth forged another vital new friendship this year. In either July or August he met Sir George Beaumont in Keswick. Beaumont was a wealthy landowner; more importantly he was a patron and lover of the arts, and a distinguished amateur artist himself. He was also a lover of the Lake District, and had first visited the area in 1777 with the artists Joseph Farington and Thomas Hearne. Beaumont's circle of friends included Sir Thomas Lawrence, John Constable, David Wilkie and Benjamin West, but even in this distinguished company Wordsworth seems to have made a particular impression, for Beaumont made the poet a remarkably generous gift – a parcel of land at Applethwaite, near Keswick. Over the coming years he and Lady Beaumont were the most faithful of friends, and tireless advocates of Wordsworth's poetry.

At the end of the year Coleridge arrived at Dove Cottage. By now, the extent of his decline was painfully apparent: 'I must tell you about Coleridge', Dorothy wrote to Catherine Clarkson in January 1804: 'two or three days before [he] was lame with the gout, stomach-sick, haunted by ugly dreams, screamed out in the night, durst not sleep etc etc …' That March, in a final bid to rescue his health, Coleridge sailed to Malta. The Wordsworths were not not to see him for another two years.

In the weeks leading up to Coleridge's departure, Dorothy and Mary had busily copied all Wordsworth's unpublished poems into a notebook, 'to be his companions in Italy'. Throughout this last year Wordsworth had been producing new poetry at an astonishing rate. He had finished the 'Ode, Intimations of Immortality', written the 'Ode to Duty', and composed perhaps his most famous poem, 'I wandered lonely as a cloud'. Above all, he had returned to the autobiographical verses begun years ago at Goslar. In 1799 he had composed a two-book version of the poem, now known to us as the *Prelude*, but then referred to simply as the 'Poem to Coleridge'. In Grasmere he expanded this into a much more

William Wordsworth

ambitious work. His theme, intended as an introduction to 'The Recluse', was nothing less than the growth of his own mind. In magnificently assured verse Wordsworth traced the guiding forces that had shaped his adult life: from his childhood in Cockermouth and schooldays in Hawkshead, to Cambridge and the Alps, Wales, London, and revolutionary France:

> *Of genius, power,*
> *Creation and divinity itself,*
> *I have been speaking, for my theme has been*
> *What passed within me. Not of outward things*
> *Done visibly for other minds—words, signs*
> *Symbols or actions—but of my own heart*
> *Have I been speaking, and my youthful mind …*
> *This is in truth heroic argument*

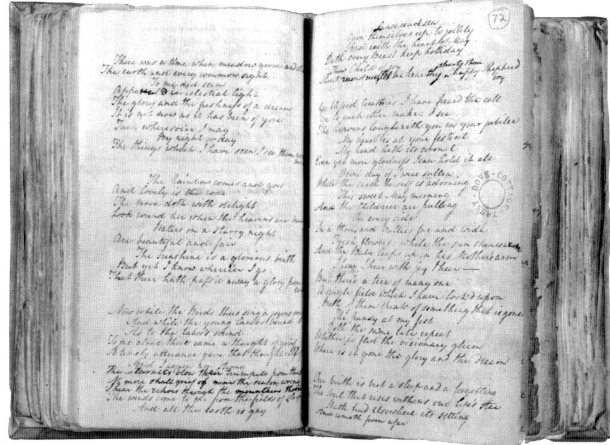

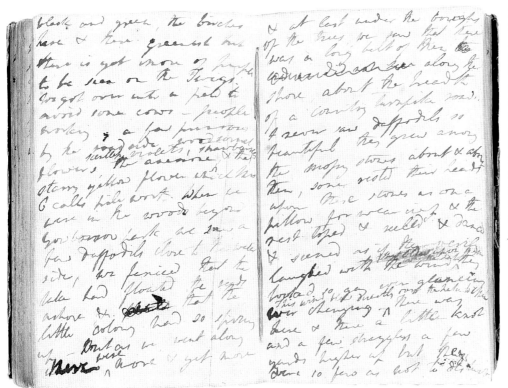

By the spring of 1804 Wordsworth had completed a five-book version of the poem.

In August Wordsworth and Mary's second child, a daughter, was born. Christened Dorothy, she was always known to the family as Dora. 'She is her Father's darling', Dorothy wrote to Lady Beaumont in September. 'She wins her way into all our hearts.' But the following year their happiness gave way to sorrow. On 5 February 1805 John Wordsworth's ship, the *Earl of Abergavenny*, had struck rocks off Portland Bill on the Dorset coast, and had sunk during the night. Fewer than half of the 387 passengers and crew had survived, and John Wordsworth, who stayed at his command, had not been among them. The news of his death came to the family at Grasmere like 'a thunderstroke'. John had been, for Wordsworth, 'a poet in every thing but words'. 'I never wrote a line without a thought of its giving him pleasure', he told Losh soon after John's death. 'My writings printed and manuscript were his delight.' The intimate circle that had grown up around Dove Cottage was now

William Wordsworth

Wordsworth's most famous poem, 'I wandered lonely as a cloud', written in 1804.

The British Library, Add.MS 47864, f.80

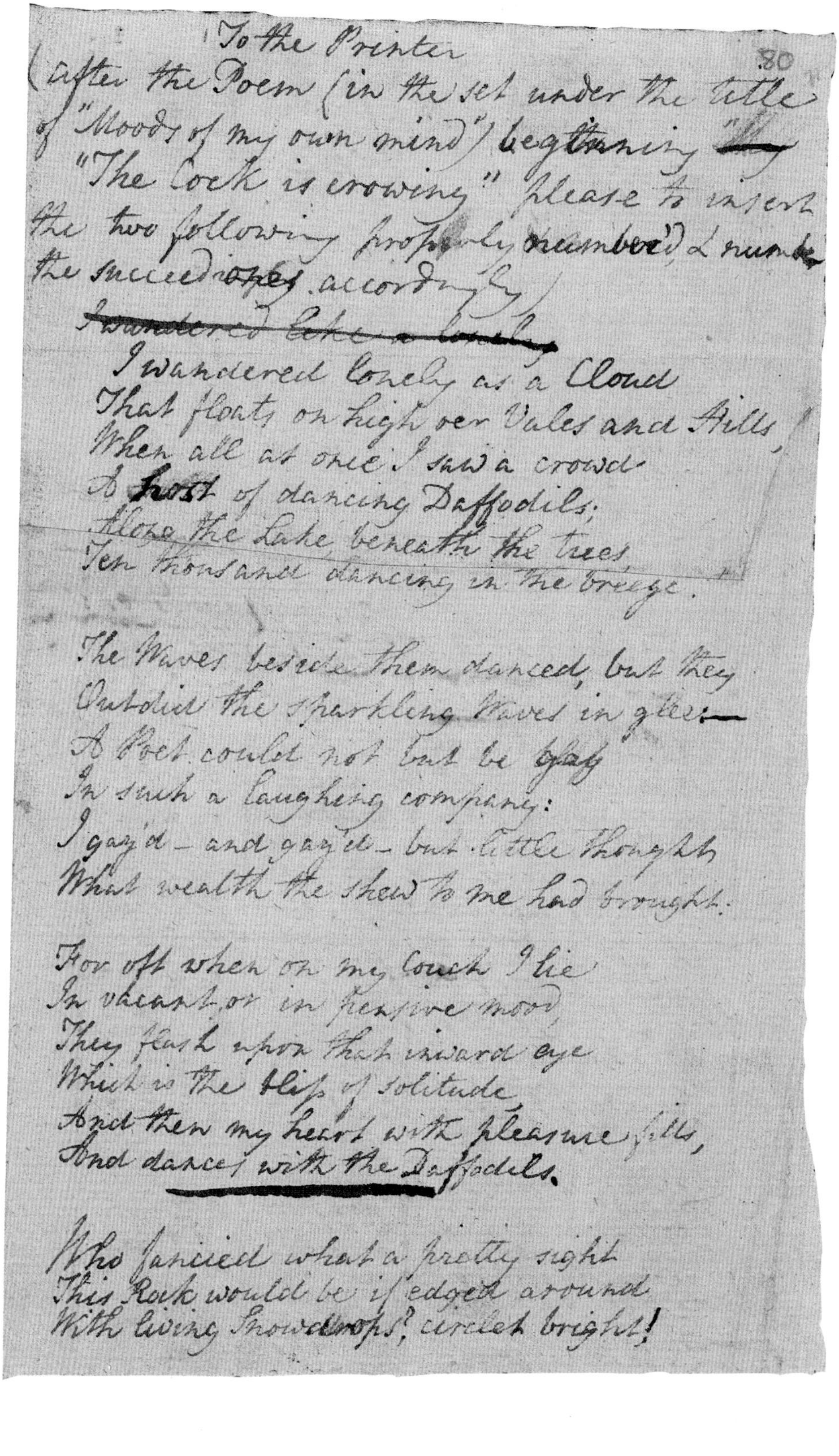

To the Printer

(after the Poem (in the set under the title of "Moods of my own mind") beginning

"The Cock is crowing" please to insert the two following properly numberd, & number the succeeding ones accordingly)

~~I wandered like a cloud~~

I wandered lonely as a Cloud
That floats on high oer Vales and Hills,
When all at once I saw a crowd
A **host** of dancing Daffodils;
Along the Lake beneath the trees
Ten thousand dancing in the breeze.

The Waves beside them danced, but they
Outdid the sparkling waves in glee:—
A Poet could not but be gay
In such a laughing company:
I gaz'd — and gaz'd — but little thought
What wealth the shew to me had brought.

For oft when on my couch I lie
In vacant, or in pensive mood,
They flash upon that inward eye
Which is the bliss of solitude
And then my heart with pleasure fills,
And dances with the Daffodils.

Who fancied what a pretty sight
This Rock would be if edged around
With living Snowdrops? circlet bright!

broken. 'For myself', Wordsworth wrote, 'I feel that there is something cut out of my life which cannot be restored.'

In May, Wordsworth completed a final, thirteen-book version of *The Prelude*. It was his finest achievement as a poet, but all he felt was dejection. 'It was not a happy day for me', he confessed to Sir George Beaumont a fortnight later, '...when I looked back upon the performance it seemed to have a dead weight about it, the reality so far short of the expectation ... above all, many heavy thoughts of my poor departed Brother hung upon me; the joy which I should have had in shewing him the Manuscript and a thousand other vain fancies and dreams.'

The wreck of the Earl of Abergavenny *off the south coast of England on 5 February 1805, in which over half the passengers and crew died, including the captain, Wordsworth's brother John. Contemporary print by R. Corbauld.*

Wordsworth Trust

≈ *Dove Cottage: 1805-8*

The memory of John continued to haunt Wordsworth. In June 1805 he and a friend went fishing at Grisedale Tarn. It was here, in September 1800, that he and Dorothy had said to goodbye to John as he left Grasmere for the last time. Overcome by the memory, Wordsworth parted from his companion in tears. In April and May the following year he was in London. There he met the Whig leader Charles James Fox and the artists Joseph Farington, David Wilkie and James Northcote. He saw old friends like Godwin, Montagu and Lamb, and had his portrait taken by the fashionable portrait painter Henry Edridge. But he spent most

William Wordsworth by society portrait painter Henry Edridge, made when the poet was thirty-six.

of his time with Sir George and Lady Beaumont at their home in Grosvenor Square, and there he saw a picture by Beaumont, *Peele Castle in a Storm*, which again brought to mind John's death. The poem he was then inspired to write, the great 'Elegiac Stanzas', finds, amidst grief, a kind of consolation:

> *But welcome fortitude, and patient chear,*
> *And frequent sights of what is to be borne!*
> *Such sights, or worse, as are before me here. –*
> *Not without hope we suffer and we mourn.*

Wordsworth's inkstand with Sara Hutchinson's quillpen.

Wordsworth Trust

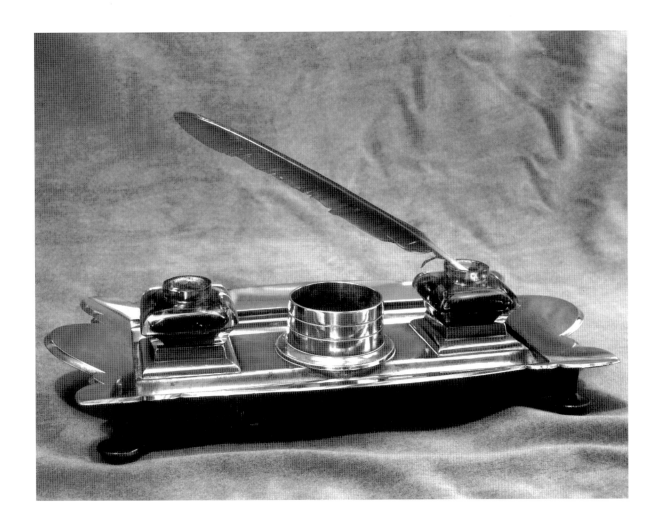

At the end of May Wordsworth was back in Grasmere, and shortly after his return his third child, Thomas, was born. Life at Dove Cottage, from a practical point of view, was becoming difficult. As many as nine people now had to live and sleep in its half-dozen rooms. In 1804, after Dora's birth, Dorothy had described the cottage as 'sadly crowded'. Now, she said, they were 'crammed in our little nest edge full ... Every bed lodges two persons at present'. Fortunately, a temporary solution offered itself in the autumn, when the Beaumonts invited the Wordsworths to winter at their country estate, Coleorton, in Leicestershire.

On 26 October 1806 the entire family left Dove Cottage for Leicestershire. On the first night of their journey, in Kendal, they had a long wished-for, but ultimately upsetting reunion. Coleridge had returned to England in August, but had delayed his journey north for two months. Now, after the long separation, the Wordsworths found a figure they barely recognized. 'We all went thither to him', wrote Dorothy, 'and never did I feel such a shock as at first sight of him. His fatness has quite changed him – it is more like the flesh of a person in a dropsy than one in health; his eyes are lost in it.' In conversation they found Coleridge reserved and impersonal, continually changing the subject 'to anything but what we were yearning after'. Wordsworth lamented this sad change in his poem 'A Complaint':

> *What happy moments did I count!*
> *Blessed was I then all bliss above!*
> *Now, for this, consecrated Fount*
> *Of murmuring, sparkling, living love,*
> *What have I? Shall I dare to tell?*
> *A comfortless, and hidden WELL*

But they invited Coleridge to join them in Leicestershire, which he did, with his son Hartley, in December.

The Wordsworths were at Coleorton for almost eight months. Beaumont was rebuilding the main house, and had asked Wordsworth to design a new winter garden. In the last few years Wordsworth had transformed the garden at Dove Cottage, and this was an opportunity for him to exercise his considerable skills as a

gardener. In the evenings, the family gathered by the fireside, and Wordsworth read them lines from *The Prelude*. Coleridge, by now, according to Dorothy, 'much more like his own old self', was overwhelmed by the poem. He wrote a reply, 'To William Wordsworth', in which he expressed his immense admiration for Wordsworth both as a poet and a friend:

> *And when O Friend! My comforter and guide!*
> *Strong in thyself, and powerful to give strength! –*
> *Thy long sustained Song finally closed,*
> *And thy deep voice had ceased – yet thou thyself*
> *Wert still before my eyes, and round us both*
> *That happy vision of beloved faces –*
> *Scarce conscious, and yet conscious of its close*
> *I sate, my being blended in one thought*
> *(Thought was it? or aspiration? or resolve?)*
> *Absorbed, yet hanging still upon the sound –*
> *And when I rose, I found myself in prayer.*

While he was at Coleorton Wordsworth also worked on his first publication since the second edition of *Lyrical Ballads*. That winter and spring the whole household, including Coleridge, helped him prepare his new volume of poetry for the press, and in April 1807 *Poems, in Two Volumes* was published. It contained the best of Wordsworth's later poems at Dove Cottage. Alongside a multitude of exquisite lyrics are some of his greatest works: the 'Sonnets dedicated to Liberty' written in 1802 after his return from Calais, 'Resolution and Independence', 'Ode to Duty', the 'Immortality Ode', 'Elegiac Stanzas', in all over a hundred new poems. But the reviews were, almost without exception, hostile. 'A more rash and injudicious speculation on the weakness or the depravity of the public taste has seldom been made', wrote James Montgomery in the *Eclectic Review*. Byron called the poetry 'namby-pamby', and Francis Jeffrey, in the *Edinburgh Review*, condemned Wordsworth's rustic subject matter as 'low, silly, or uninteresting'. 'My flesh is as insensible as iron to these petty stings', Wordsworth declared to Lady Beaumont, but he was, in truth, severely shaken. He was not to publish another volume for seven years.

The Wordsworths arrived back in Grasmere in July 1807, after a lengthy journey home through Halifax and the Yorkshire Dales. They found the valley sadly changed. 'On our arrival here our spirits sank', wrote Dorothy, 'and our first walk in the evening was very melancholy. Many persons are dead … all the trees in Bainrigg are cut down …'. That winter, the cottage received one of its last visitors, the writer Thomas De Quincey. As a seventeen year-old, Thomas De Quincey had written an effusive letter of praise to Wordsworth, and in reply had received a polite invitation to come to Grasmere. Now aged twenty-one, he had finally plucked up the courage to accept the offer. Years later, he wrote a wonderful description of his initial impressions of the cottage. He described a 'very prettily wainscotted' front room, with a single window 'with little diamond panes, embowered, at almost every season of the year, with roses; and, in the summer and autumn, with a profusion of jessamine and other fragrant shrubs'. Mary Wordsworth, he wrote, was 'a tall young woman, with the most winning expression of benignity upon her features that I ever beheld', while Dorothy was 'a lady, much shorter, much slighter … Her face was of Egyptian brown; rarely, in a woman of English birth, had I seen a more determinate gipsy tan. Her eyes were not soft, as Mrs. Wordsworth's nor were they fierce and bold, but they were wild and startling, and hurried in their motion.'

It was the family's last winter at Dove Cottage. In May 1808, with great regret, they were forced move to a larger house, Allan Bank, on the other side of the lake.

❧ *Grasmere: 1808-13*

Allan Bank was a large white house standing just above Grasmere village. As a piece of local architecture, Wordsworth despised it. In 1805 he had watched it being built for a Liverpool lawyer, 'a wretched creature … of the name of Crump', and had written to a friend in dismay: 'When you next enter the sweet Paradise of Grasmere you will see staring you in the face, upon that beautiful ridge that elbows out into the vale (behind the church and towering far above its steeple) a temple of abomination … this House will stare you in the face from every part of the Vale, and entirely destroy its character of simplicity and seclusion.' Once he had moved in, he soon discovered that Allan Bank had a more practical shortcoming: it was exposed on all sides to the winds, and as a result the chimneys smoked badly, so badly that in stormy weather most of the rooms were uninhabitable. On one particularly rough night the family had to retreat to the least affected room, Wordsworth's study, and even then were unable to see each other for the smoke.

What Allan Bank could provide, however, was space. With a wife and three children, a sister, a sister-in-law, and servants, Wordsworth now had a large household, and it was about to become larger still. At the beginning of September Coleridge appeared, and stayed with the Wordsworths, on and off, for the next two years. His young sons, Hartley and Berkeley, went to school in neighbouring Ambleside, and spent their weekends at Allan Bank. Later that month Wordsworth's second daughter, Catherine, was born. Finally, in November, Thomas De Quincey arrived. He became a much-loved addition to the family, and was a great favourite with the children, but he remained in awe of Wordsworth and Coleridge; 'he is a good-tempered amiable creature & uncommonly clever & an excellent scholar', wrote Sara Hutchinson to a friend, 'but he is very shy & so reverences Wm and C that he chats very little but is content to listen'.

For the first year and a half at Allan Bank, Wordsworth was largely preoccupied with prose works. He had lost none of his interest in public affairs (indeed, in 1833 he remarked that 'he had given twelve hours' thought to the condition and prospects of society, for one to poetry'), and his first project

Opposite page:

Allan Bank in Grasmere as it is today. The Wordsworths moved here from Dove Cottage in the summer of 1808, and stayed until 1811.

Alex Black

81

was a political pamphlet. One event monopolised his attention. In August 1808 the British had defeated Napoleon's army at the Battle of Vimiero in Portugal. After the victory they had agreed, in an arrangement known as the 'Convention of Cintra', to transport the defeated French back to France in British ships, and give them back to Napoleon. Many people in England, including Wordsworth, saw this as an affront to the Portuguese and Spanish struggle for liberty. 'It would not be easy to conceive with what a depth of feeling I entered into the struggle carried on by the Spaniards for their deliverance from the usurped power of the French', Wordsworth later recalled. In November, after an unsuccessful attempt to call a public meeting of protest, he began his pamphlet, and for the next few months thought of little else. '[It] occupies all his thoughts', wrote Dorothy, 'his first and last thoughts are of Spain and Portugal.' Coleridge's daughter Sara, who visited Allan Bank that autumn, later wrote in her *Memoir*: 'How gravely and earnestly used Samuel Taylor Coleridge and William Wordsworth and my uncle Southey also to discuss the affairs of the nation, as if it all came home to their business and bosoms, as if it were their private concern!'

In February 1809 the pamphlet, entitled *The Convention of Cintra*, was ready for publication, and De Quincey left for London to see it through the press. This was an unenviable task, for Wordsworth, as was his habit, insisted on making life as difficult for the printer as possible. In the coming weeks, corrections, additions and proofs passed between London and Grasmere regularly, and De Quincey found himself, as Coleridge put it, 'blown about by the changeful winds of an anxious Author's second thoughts'. When *The Convention of Cintra* finally appeared at the end of May 1809 public interest had died down, and sales were disappointing. Wordsworth himself was diffident about the work: 'It is indeed very imperfect', he wrote to Francis Wrangham, 'and will, I fear, be little read; but, if it is real, it cannot I hope fail of doing some good, though I am aware it will create me a world of enemies, and call forth the old yell of Jacobinism.'

Meanwhile, Coleridge was busy with a new venture. On 1 June he published the first issue of a weekly periodical, *The Friend, A Literary, Moral and Political Weekly Paper*, written and promoted entirely by himself. Over the next ten months, with Sara Hutchinson acting as his secretary and amanuensis, he published a further twenty-six issues. This was an extraordinary achievement, and one which surprised many, not least Wordsworth, who now thought Coleridge, through a fundamental weakness of character, incapable of sustained activity. Three days before the publication of the first issue of *The Friend* he had written highly critically to their old friend Thomas Poole: 'Coleridge neither will nor can execute anything of important benefit either to himself his family or mankind. Neither his talents nor his genius mighty as they are nor his vast information will avail him anything; they are all frustrated by a derangement in his intellectual and moral constitution.'

When *The Friend* did, after all, appear, Wordsworth helped by contributing two substantial pieces to the journal. The first, *Reply to Mathetes*, was a response to a letter in *The Friend* from Alexander Blair and John Wilson (later famous as 'Christopher North' of *Blackwoods* magazine, and a future Professor of Moral Philosophy at Edinburgh University), and concerned itself with the education of the young. The proper calling of youth, Wordsworth concluded, is 'not to analyze with scrupulous minuteness, but to accumulate in genial confidence; its instinct, its safety, its benefit, its glory, is to love, to admire, to feel'. The second piece, which appeared in the final issue of *The Friend* on 15 March 1810, was the first of his three *Essays upon Epitaphs*. Here, as he considered the nature of the epitaph, Wordsworth touched upon those intimations of immortality that informed his greatest poetry: 'without the consciousness of a principle of immortality in the human soul', he wrote, 'Man could

First published in 1810 as the preface to Wilkinson's Select Views in Cumberland, Westmoreland and Lancashire, *and steadily enlarged and revised in successive new editions, Wordsworth's description of the English Lake District became the most popular and influential guidebook to the area.*

The British Library, 579.a.5

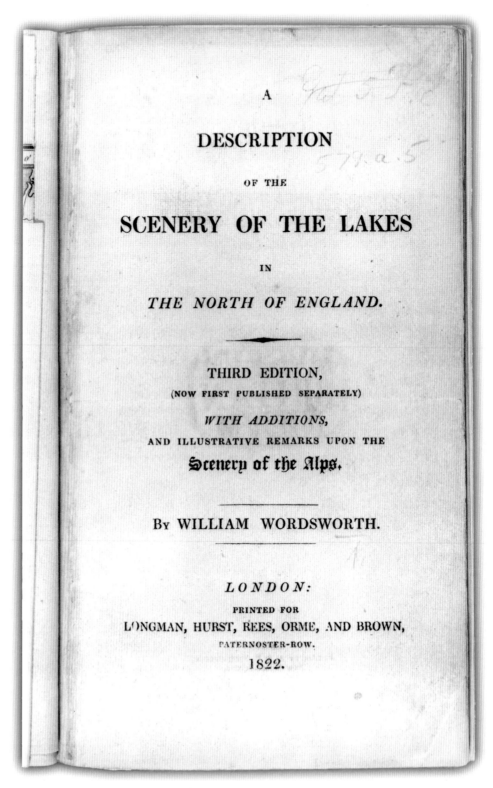

A

DESCRIPTION

OF THE

SCENERY OF THE LAKES

IN

THE NORTH OF ENGLAND.

THIRD EDITION,
(NOW FIRST PUBLISHED SEPARATELY)

WITH ADDITIONS,

AND ILLUSTRATIVE REMARKS UPON THE

𝕾𝖈𝖊𝖓𝖊𝖗𝖞 𝖔𝖋 𝖙𝖍𝖊 𝕬𝖑𝖕𝖘.

BY WILLIAM WORDSWORTH.

LONDON:
PRINTED FOR
LONGMAN, HURST, REES, ORME, AND BROWN,
PATERNOSTER-ROW.
1822.

never have had awakened in him the desire to live in the remembrance of his fellows: mere love, or the yearning of kind towards kind, could not have produced it.'

One other major prose work dates from Wordsworth's time at Allan Bank. In 1809 a clergyman from the north east of England, the Reverend Joseph Wilkinson, asked Wordsworth if he would contribute an introduction to a book of engravings made after his own watercolours, *Select Views in Cumberland, Westmorland, and Lancashire*. Wordsworth hesitated at first, as he had a decidedly low opinion of Wilkinson's drawings, but the introduction that he eventually wrote was published in 1810. Over the years, this was to grow and develop until it became one of his best-known (and best-selling) works: *A Guide through the District of the Lakes*. Here, Wordsworth lovingly described his native scenery, and first articulated the idea that the Lake District should be a national park, referring to 'persons of pure taste throughout the whole island, who, by their visits (often repeated) to the Lakes in the North of England, testify that they deem the district a sort of national property, in which every man has a right and interest who has an eye to perceive and a heart to enjoy'.

All this literary activity could not, however, disguise the fact that by 1810 life at Allan Bank had become extremely difficult. Despite its size, the house was crowded, and Coleridge was moody and withdrawn. In the past, the Wordsworths had been confident in their ability to raise their friend's spirits; experience had since taught them otherwise. Shortly before moving into Allan Bank Dorothy had confessed to Catherine Clarkson: 'We had long experience at Coleorton that it was not in our power to make him happy.' Now, two years later, she wrote again to Catherine Clarkson: 'We have no hope of him – none that he will ever do anything more than he had already done.' Coleridge rarely emerged from his room, she said, and when he did appear, at mealtimes, was 'impatient to get back to his solitude. He goes the moment his food is swallowed. Sometimes he does not speak a word.' Nothing, not even the finest spring day, could persuade him to leave the house: 'this beautiful valley seems a blank to him'. His continuing love for Sara Hutchinson Dorothy condemned as 'no more than a fanciful dream'.

Everyone needed breathing space. In March, Sara Hutchinson, worn out by her constant work on *The Friend*, and made ill by Coleridge's persistent, hopeless devotion, left Allan Bank for her brother Tom's farm in Wales. In May, Coleridge himself left for Keswick. Later that month, Mary gave birth to her fifth and final child, William, and in July Wordsworth and Dorothy travelled south to stay with the Beaumonts at Coleorton. It was a welcome respite, but a brief one, for that autumn the tension between Wordsworth and Coleridge developed into an open quarrel.

At beginning of September, Wordsworth returned north. Later that month he was joined at Allan Bank by Basil Montagu. Montagu had heard of Coleridge's condition, and confidently believed that he could provide him with the 'tranquillity' he needed. Coleridge, still in Keswick, agreed to return with Montagu to London, and on 18 October arrived at Allan Bank. After a brief conversation with Wordsworth, he and Montagu proceeded south. In the meantime, however, Wordsworth had tried to convince Montagu that his confidence was misplaced; 'William used many arguments to persuade M. that his purpose of keeping Coleridge comfortable could not be answered by their being in the same house together', Dorothy explained to Catherine Clarkson some time later, 'but in vain … After this William spoke out and told M the nature of C's habits.' Once they were in London, Montagu told Coleridge that he had been 'commissioned' to repeat what Wordsworth had said. According to Coleridge, when he recalled the incident later, this was that he was 'a rotten drunkard' and 'an absolute nuisance to the family', who was 'rotting out his entrails with intemperance'. Coleridge was deeply hurt. It was the start of a long and painful estrangement.

In the summer of 1811 the Wordsworths left Allan Bank, and moved into the rectory next to Grasmere church. 'We like our new house very much', Dorothy told Catherine Clarkson in June, '… William's parlour is but a little cabin; but it will be very snug and neat, when we have got the furniture put into it.' After his digression into prose, Wordsworth was again writing poetry, and had returned to *The Recluse*. For the first time, however, he was unable to share his great work with Coleridge – the two friends were refusing to speak to each other. In February 1812 Coleridge travelled through Grasmere on his way to Keswick, and even then he did not stop and call at the rectory. In May, after Wordsworth had travelled to London 'with a *determination* to confront Coleridge and Montagu upon this vile business', they finally put aside their differences, but the intimacy of earlier years was never to return.

While Wordsworth was in the south, tragedy struck at home. His daughter Catherine had never been strong. In April 1810 she had been seized by a violent convulsive fit that had left her partly paralysed. Two years later, on the evening of 3 June, Catherine was again seized by convulsions, and died early the following morning, aged only four. It was almost a week before Wordsworth received the news and, by chance, his wife was also away from Grasmere, so only Dorothy, Sara Hutchinson and Wordsworth's son John were able to attend the funeral. 'It is a great addition to our affliction that her Father and Mother were not here to witness her last struggles', Dorothy wrote when breaking the news to Thomas De Quincey, 'and to see her in the last happy weeks of her short life.' Then, in December, the Wordsworths' second son, the six year-old, 'heavenly-tempered' Thomas, died of pneumonia after contracting measles. 'I dare not say in what state of mind I am', Wordsworth wrote to Robert Southey. 'I loved the Boy with all with the utmost love of which my soul is capable, and he is taken from me.'

A year later, the memory of Catherine inspired Wordsworth to write one of his most moving sonnets:

Surprized by joy – impatient as the Wind

I wished to share the transport – Oh! with whom

But Thee, long buried in the silent Tomb,

That spot which no vicissitude can find?

Love, faithful love recalled thee to my mind –

But how could I forget thee! – Through what power

Even for the least division of an hour,

Have I been so beguiled as to be blind

To my most grievous loss? – That thought's return

Was the worst pang that sorrow ever bore,

Save one, one only, when I stood forlorn,

Knowing my heart's best treasure was no more;

That neither present time, nor years unborn

Could to my sight that heavenly face restore

❧ *Rydal Mount: 1813-15*

In the weeks following Thomas's death Wordsworth's one concern was the wellbeing of his bereaved family. Two things were clear to him. First, he had to achieve some measure of financial security. Second, the family had to leave Grasmere. The rectory was dark and damp, and held too many memories; 'wherever we look we are reminded of some pretty action of those innnocent Children', Dorothy told Mrs Cookson at the end of year, 'especially Thomas whose life latterly has been connected with the church-yard in the most affecting manner – there he played daily amongst his schoolfellows, and daily tripped through it to school, a place which was his pride and delight.'

The Scottish writer James Hogg. Hogg met Wordsworth during the latter's tour of Scotland in 1814, and later came to stay at Rydal Mount. His death in 1835 inspired one of Wordsworth's finest late poems, 'Extempore effusion upon the Death of James Hogg'. Drawing by William Bewick, 1824.

Scottish National Portrait Gallery

Financial help came soon. In 1802 the family's old enemy, the Earl of Lonsdale, had died, and within a year his heir, Sir William Lowther, a much more reasonable man, had agreed to repay the money that had been owed to the Wordsworths since their father's death in 1783. Now, learning of Wordsworth's circumstances, Sir William offered the poet £100 a year until he could find him a salaried position. After some hesitation, Wordsworth accepted this generous offer, 'until the office becomes vacant, or any other change takes place in my circumstances which might render it unnecessary'. To his relief, he did not have to wait long; in April 1813, he was appointed Distributor of Stamps for Westmorland and part of Cumberland. As such, he was responsible for collecting the taxes payable on all legal documents created in the district, and sending them down to the Board of Stamps in London. It was a job he was to perform diligently for almost thirty years.

This improvement in Wordsworth's fortunes enabled him, at last, to leave the rectory, and in May he and his family moved to the neighbouring village of Rydal. Their new home, Rydal Mount, delighted them. It was roomy and comfortable, and had a clear view over Rydal Water towards Loughrigg Fell. There was a good-sized garden, which they set about developing with their usual skill.

The move to Rydal Mount, and Wordsworth's employment, marked the beginning of a new lifestyle, one very different from the austere years at Dove Cottage. 'You stare', Dorothy wrote self-consciously to Catherine Clarkson, 'and the simplicity of the dear Town End cottage comes before your eyes, and you are tempted to say: "Are they changed, are they setting up for fine folks? For making parties, giving Dinners etc etc?"' There were some who thought that in accepting the patronage of Sir William Lowther, and working as a civil servant, Wordsworth was somehow betraying his earlier ideal of the independent poet. In 1812 the young Percy Bysshe Shelley had visited the Lake District, and noted: 'Wordsworth … yet retains the integrity of his independence; but his poverty is such that he is frequently obliged to beg for a shirt to his back.' One suspects that William Wordsworth, Distributor of Stamps and tenant of Rydal Mount, would have left Shelley unimpressed. But for Wordsworth it was a practical decision: he wished to provide his family with security, and he could never hope to do that purely as a poet. 'My employment I find salutary to me', he wrote to Francis Wrangham in August 1813, 'and of consequence in a pecuniary point of view, as my *Literary* employments bring me no emolument, nor promise any.'

In the summer of 1814 Wordsworth and Mary, together with their son John and Sara Hutchinson, toured Scotland. Their route north took them through Glasgow, the Trossachs and Glencoe, and by the middle of August they had reached as far as Inverness. On their return journey they passed through Edinburgh, and here they met one of Scotland's most celebrated writers, the poet, novelist and one-time farm labourer, James Hogg. Wordsworth, according to Hogg, was 'clothed in a grey russet jacket and pantaloons, be it remembered, and wore a broad-brimmed beaver hat; so that to strangers he doubtless had a very original appearance ... all the while he was in Scotland I loved him better and better'. Hogg met up with the Wordsworths further south at Traquair, and introduced them to his favourite landscape around the River Yarrow. Wordsworth, he later recalled, 'was in great good humour, delightful and most eloquent'.

While he was in Scotland, Wordsworth's latest poem, *The Excursion*, was published. This was his first published poetry since *Poems in Two Volumes* in 1807, and was Miltonic in both its length – almost eight thousand lines of blank verse – and its ambition. It began with a revised version of the poem that Wordsworth had begun at Racedown, 'The Ruined Cottage', and developed into a long philosophical debate between the poem's principal characters: the Wanderer, philosophical, closely attached to nature; the Solitary, pessimistic, disillusioned; and the Pastor, strong in religious faith. Even physically the book was imposing: a beautifully produced quarto volume highly priced at two guineas.

But if *The Excursion* was Wordsworth's most ambitious work to date, it also announced to the public his wider, still unrealized ambition – 'The Recluse'. *The Excursion* was only 'a portion' of this great work. 'Several years ago', Wordsworth wrote in the preface, 'when the Author retired to his native mountains, in the hope of being enabled to construct a literary work that might live, it was a reasonable thing that he should take a review of his own mind, and examine how far Nature and Education had qualified him for such employment.' This 'review' was the as yet unpublished

The Excursion, 1814, was one of Wordsworth's most ambitious publications, but was published as only 'a portion' of an even larger work, 'The Recluse'.

The British Library, C116.g.3

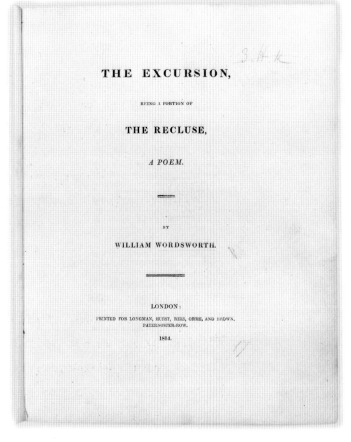

THE EXCURSION,

BEING A PORTION OF

THE RECLUSE,

A POEM.

BY

WILLIAM WORDSWORTH.

LONDON:
PRINTED FOR LONGMAN, HURST, REES, ORME, AND BROWN,
PATERNOSTER-ROW.
1814.

Prelude, and, echoing the letter he had written to Losh sixteen years ago, Wordsworth went on to say that 'the result of the investigation which gave rise to it was a determination to compose a philosophical poem, containing views of Man, Nature and Society; and to be entitled, the Recluse; as having for its principal subject the sensations and opinions of a poet living in retirement.' In an extended metaphor, Wordsworth then described his life's work: taking the form of a gothic church, he saw the *Prelude* as 'the ante-chapel', and the *Excursion* as the 'body'. His many smaller poems, 'minor Pieces, which have been long before the Public', were 'the little cells, or oratories, and sepuchral recesses, ordinarily included in those edifices'. He

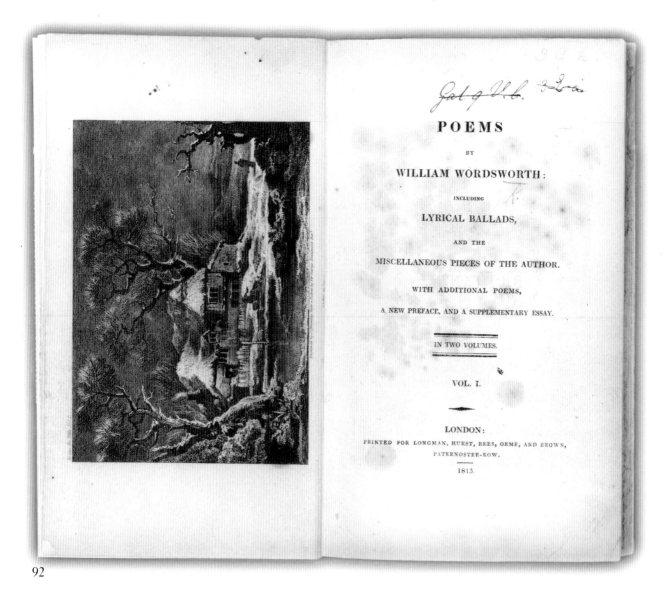

POEMS

BY

WILLIAM WORDSWORTH:

INCLUDING

LYRICAL BALLADS,

AND THE

MISCELLANEOUS PIECES OF THE AUTHOR.

WITH ADDITIONAL POEMS,

A NEW PREFACE, AND A SUPPLEMENTARY ESSAY.

IN TWO VOLUMES.

VOL. I.

LONDON:
PRINTED FOR LONGMAN, HURST, REES, ORME, AND BROWN,
PATERNOSTER-ROW.
1815.

concluded with a 'Prospectus', part of the poem he had written when he first arrived at Dove Cottage, 'Home at Grasmere'.

A year after *The Excursion* Wordsworth further consolidated his poetic achievement with two more publications. First, he collected his shorter poetry into two volumes, extensively revised, and arranged not chronologically, but into themes such as 'Poems Founded on the Affections', 'Poems Proceeding from Sentiment and Reflection', and 'Poems referring to the Period of Childhood', thus establishing the idea of a coherent body of work. Then he published a poem originally written in 1808, *The White Doe of Rylestone*. Like *The Excursion* this was a deluxe quarto volume, and had as its frontispiece an engraving of the poem's setting, Bolton Abbey in Yorkshire, after a picture by Sir George Beaumont, to whom the poem was dedicated. Wordsworth had dedicated *The Excursion* to his new patron, Sir William Lowther.

⟋ *Rydal Mount: 1816-20*

The *Excursion*, the *Collected Poems*, and *The White Doe of Rylestone* were Wordsworth's justification for his years of retirement in Grasmere. Together, they comprised his achievement thus far as a poet, and he hoped they would restore his reputation after the failure of *Poems in Two Volumes*. But critics and his fellow writers were disappointed, and sales were poor.

'This will never do', began Francis Jeffrey in his devastating review of *The Excursion* in the *Edinburgh Review*. 'It is longer, weaker, and tamer, than any of Mr Wordsworth's other productions; with less boldness of originality, and less even of that extreme simplicity and lowliness of tone which wavered so prettily, in the *Lyrical Ballads*, between silliness and pathos.' His review of *The White Doe of Rylestone* was similarly direct: 'This, we think, has the merit of being the very worst poem we ever saw in a quarto volume.' Jeffrey considered Wordsworth a self-indulgent mystic; his exploration of his own life and feelings was egotism, and his choice of rural subjects misguided.

Coleridge described his initial reponse to *The Excursion* in a letter to Lady Beaumont. It was, he said, inferior to the unpublished *Prelude*, and the finest lines of the poem, in Book One, were written long ago in Alfoxden. He wrote a long letter to Wordsworth explaining why he felt the poem fell short of his expectations, and two years later, in *Biographia Literaria*, he analysed what he called 'the characteristic defects of Wordsworth's poetry'.

Younger writers felt that Wordsworth (and Coleridge and Southey with him) had betrayed his early radicalism by allying himself with a reactionary Tory government and the established church. They believed that his poetry had suffered as a result. In 1817 Robert Southey's radical early poem, *Wat Tyler*, had been published against his wishes, and in reviewing the poem, William Hazlitt took the opportunity to condemn not only Southey's, but Coleridge's and Wordsworth's apostasy. For him, Wordsworth's revolutionary power as a poet had been a direct consequence of his revolutionary politics: 'Their Jacobin principles indeed gave rise to their Jacobin poetry', he wrote. 'Since they gave up the first, their poetical powers have flagged … Their genius, their style, their versification, every thing down to their spelling, was revolutionary.' Wordsworth, like Coleridge and Southey, had lost his 'romantic enthusiasm' to 'vulgar ambition'.

Lord Byron had never liked Wordsworth's poetry, and the publication of *The Excursion* only confirmed his dislike. In a letter to the poet and journalist Leigh Hunt he called Wordsworth 'this arch-apostle of mystery and mysticism'; 'there is undoubtedly much natural talent spilt over "the Excursion"', he said, 'but it is rain upon rocks—where it stands & stagnates—or rain upon sands where it falls without fertilizing—who can understand him?—let those who do make him intelligible.' In *Don Juan* he wrote:

> *Wordsworth's last quarto, by the way, is bigger*
> *Than any since the birthday of typography;*
> *A drowsy frowzy poem called the 'Excursion,'*
> *Writ in a manner which is my aversion.*

Percy Bysshe Shelley was far more influenced by Wordsworth's poetry than Byron. Indeed, Byron complained that Shelley had once tried to convert him to it: 'Shelley', he wrote to Thomas Medwin, 'when I was in Switzerland, used to dose me with Wordsworth physic even to nausea; and I do remember reading some things of his with pleasure.' *The Excursion*, however, was a disappointment. 'Shelley … brings home Wordsworth's Excursion, of which we read a part', Mary Shelley noted in her journal in 1814, 'much disappointed. He is a slave.' Two years later Shelley published a sonnet, 'To Wordsworth', expressing his feeling of betrayal:

Percy Bysshe Shelley was strongly influenced by Wordsworth's poetry, but was disappointed by the elder poet's conservatism in later life. Drawing after a portrait by Amelia Curran, 1819.

William Wordsworth

Thou wert as a lone star, whose light did shine

On some frail bark in winter's midnight roar:

Thou hast like to a rock-built refuge stood

Above the blind and battling multitude:

In honoured poverty thy voice did weave

Song consecrate to truth and liberty, –

Deserting these, thou leavest me to grieve,

Thus having been, that thou shouldst cease to be.

But for one young poet, John Keats, *The Excursion* was one of the 'three things to rejoice at in this Age'. In 1816 he sent a sonnet to a friend of Wordsworth's, the historical painter Benjamin Robert Haydon, 'Great spirits on earth now are sojourning'. Here he described Wordsworth as 'He of the cloud, the cataract, the lake / Who on Helvellyn's summit wide awake / catches his freshness from Archangel's wing'. When Haydon offered to send the poem to Wordsworth, Keats confessed: 'the very idea of your sending this to Wordsworth puts me out of breath'. Keats and Wordsworth finally met in London in 1817, and in January the following year Keats was telling his friend Benjamin Bailey that he was seeing 'a great deal' of the older poet. He characterized Wordsworth's poetry brilliantly as the 'egotistical sublime', and thought him 'deeper than Milton' in his capacity to 'look into the human heart'. In 1818 he told Haydon: 'I am convinced there are three things to rejoice at in this Age, The Excursion, Your Pictures and Hazlitt's depth of taste.'

Even Keats was surprised, however, when, walking through the Lakes in 1818, he discovered that Wordsworth was canvassing rigorously for the Tories in the local elections against the liberal Whig Henry Brougham. 'Wordsworth versus Brougham!!' he wrote to his brother Tom. 'Sad – sad – sad – and yet the family has been his friend always. What can we say?'

Wordsworth's political activity also worried his family: 'Poetry & all good & great things will be lost in Electioneering', complained Sara Hutchinson. But the following year he was publishing again: 'Peter Bell', a poem written at Alfoxden, and 'Benjamin the Waggoner'. The sales of the former benefited from a parody by John Hamilton Reynolds, which had ingeniously contrived to appear before the poem

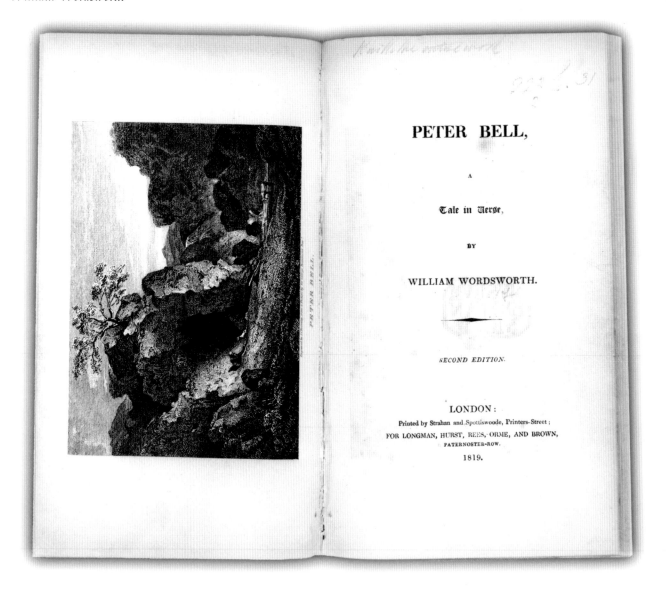

itself. In 1819 he published a sonnet sequence, *The River Duddon*, and for once the reviews were almost universally favourable, and sales good. The last poem in the sequence is justly famous:

> *I thought of Thee, my partner and my guide,*
> *As being past away.—Vain sympathies!*
> *For, backward, Duddon, as I cast my eyes,*
> *I see what was, and is, and will abide;*

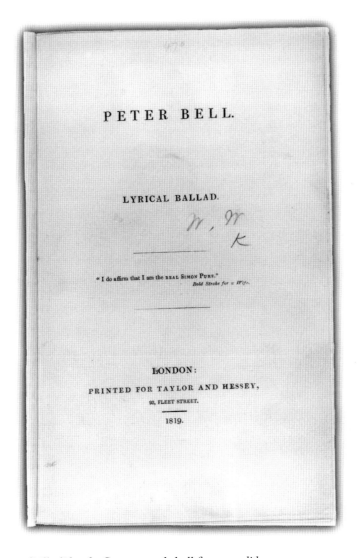

Peter Bell *was written at Alfoxden in 1798, but not published until 1819 (opposite). A parody by John Hamilton Reynolds, also called* Peter Bell, *appeared shortly beforehand (left);* 'The false one is very stupid' *wrote Sara Hutchinson,* 'but I have no doubt that it has helped the sale of the true one.'

Left:

The British Library, 11642 bbb 53

Opposite page:

The British Library, C95.d.2

Still glides the Stream, and shall for ever glide;

The Form remains, the Function never dies;

While we, the brave, the mighty, and the wise,

We Men, who in our morn of youth defied

The elements, must vanish;—be it so!

Enough, if something from our hands have power

To live, and act, and serve the future hour;

And if, as toward the silent tomb we go,

Through love, through hope, and faith's transcendent dower,

We feel that we are greater than we know

Wordsworth's spectacles and case. In later life Wordsworth was plagued with eye problems.

Shortly after the *Duddon* sonnets came *The Miscellaneous Poems of William Wordsworth*. Here Wordsworth gathered together all the shorter poems he had written up to then, as if clearing the way for his major work, 'The Recluse', but Sara Hutchinson was understandably sceptical: 'he *says* he will never trouble himself with anything but the Recluse', she wrote. Wordsworth also reviewed his past in a more personal way. From July to November 1820 he, Mary and Dorothy, made a tour of Europe. They followed, quite deliberately, the steps that Wordsworth had taken through the continent thirty years before with Robert Jones. They also spent a month with Annette and Caroline in Paris. It was the first meeting between Wordsworth's wife and the mother of his first child.

⤳ *Rydal Mount: 1821-32*

I n 1821 Wordworth published *Ecclesiatical Sketches*, a sequence of over a hundred sonnets prompted by the current issue of Catholic Emancipation. Its purpose, wrote Wordsworth, 'was, as much as possible, to confine my view to the introduction, progress and operation of the church in England, both previous and subsequent to the Reformation'. The following year he published a group of poems inspired by his recent trip to Europe, *Memorials of a Tour on the Continent, 1820*, and, for the first time separately, the *Description of the Scenery of the Lakes*. But for the next ten years, Wordsworth wrote little, and published nothing new.

Instead, he threw himself into an energetic social life. For most of the next decade, Rydal Mount was packed with visitors. The Wordsworths welcomed old and

An affectionate portrait of William and Mary Wordsworth at Rydal Mount, in 1839, when they were both aged sixty-nine. Painting by Margaret Gillies.

Wordsworth Trust

new friends alike. Robert Jones, William Wilberforce, the Clarksons, and Walter Scott all came to stay. The most remarkable of Wordsworth's new friends was William Rowan Hamilton, an exceptional mathematician who, in his youthful brilliance, reminded him of Coleridge. Hamilton's wife remembered Wordsworth as having 'a slight touch of rusticity and constraint about his perfect gentlemanliness of manner which I liked … everything he said and did had an unaffected simplicity and dignity, and peacefulness of thought that were very striking.' In 1821 an army captain on half-pay called Edward Quillinan came to live in Rydal. The following year his wife died in an tragic accident and he returned to the south, but during his short residence he had formed a warm friendship with the Wordsworths, particularly Dora.

When Wordsworth wasn't entertaining, he travelled: he visited his brother Christopher, now master of Trinity College, Cambridge; he stayed with the Beaumonts at Coleorton, and was often the guest of Sir William Lowther at Lowther Castle. London was a favourite destination, for there he could both enjoy high society, and see his oldest friends: Coleridge, Lamb, Godwin and Haydon. He also travelled extensively abroad. In 1823 he toured Belgium and Holland with Mary. The following year, he, Mary and Dora were shown around North Wales by Robert Jones, and in 1828 he, Dora and Coleridge made, apparently on impulse, a tour of Belgium, the Rhineland and Holland. One observer in Belgium, Thomas Gratton, thought that Coleridge resembled a placid clergyman; Wordsworth he described, not altogether flatteringly, as 'tall, wiry, harsh in features, coarse in figure, inelegant in looks' but he noticed that he had 'a total absence of affectation or egotism', and tended to defer to Coleridge, who as usual kept up a constant stream of talk. In 1829 Wordsworth toured Ireland, staying in Dublin as the guest of William Rowan Hamilton.

In September 1831 Wordsworth wrote a letter to his friend John Kenyon. The summer, he said, had been bright and busy: 'Regattas, Balls, Dejeuners, Picnics by the Lake side, on the Islands, and on the Mountain tops – Fireworks by night – Dancing on the green sward by day – in short a fever of pleasure from morn to dewy eve – from dewy eve till break of day.' Rydal Mount had been at the centre of these festivites. In the room where he was dictating the letter, Wordsworth told Kenyon, there had just been a dance – 'forty beaus and belles, besides matrons, ancient

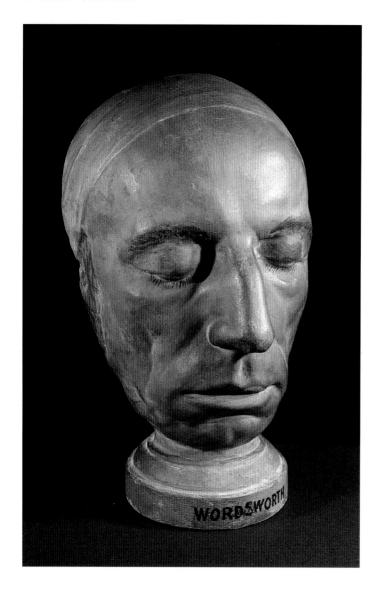

A lifemask of William Wordsworth, made by Benjamin Robert Haydon on 12 June 1815.

Spinsters, and Greybeards' – and the next day, in the same room, there was to be 'a Venison feast'. The letter gives something of the flavour of the last ten years, and shows that generally Wordsworth was in good spirits. He was over sixty, but his climbing, Dorothy said, put younger men to shame, and he was still 'the crack skater on Rydal Lake'.

But all this activity left little room for poetry. A new five-volume edition of Wordsworth's works appeared in May 1827, and four years later his first selection, *Selections from the Poems of William Wordsworth, Esq., Chiefly for the Use of Schools and Young Persons*, was published. Otherwise, Wordsworth was silent, and sometimes he felt the absence of new poems keenly. 'The Muse has foresaken me', he wrote to Haydon in 1831, 'being scared away by the villainous aspect of the Times'. Hartley Coleridge remarked that as the years passed by, Wordsworth became 'less of the Poet, and more of the respectable, talented, hospitable Country gentleman'.

In August 1831 Wordsworth and Dora visited Walter Scott at his home in Abbotsford. Scott had less than a year to live, and Wordsworth was deeply affected by the sight of his friend and fellow writer, aged and exhausted by debt and overwork: 'How sadly changed did I find him from the man I had seen so healthy, gay and hopeful, a few years before ...' he wrote. The poem he wrote memorialising that day, 'Yarrow Revisited', has the elegiac dignity that was to distinguish the best of his late poems:

And what, for this frail world, were all
That mortals do or suffer,
Did no responsive harp, no pen,
Memorial tribute offer?
Yea, what were mighty Nature's self?
Her features, could they win us,
Unhelped by the poetic voice
That hourly speaks within us.

Nor deem that localised Romance
Plays false with our affections;
Unsantifies our tears – made sport
For fanciful dejections:
Ah, no! the visions of the past
Sustain the heart in feeling,
Life as she is – our changeful Life,
With friends and kindred dealing.

The manuscript of
'Yarrow Revisited',
written in 1831
shortly after
Wordsworth's last
meeting with
Walter Scott.

Wordsworth Trust

William Wordsworth

The royal warrant declaring Wordsworth Poet Laureate to Queen Victoria, dated 6 April 1843.

Wordsworth Trust

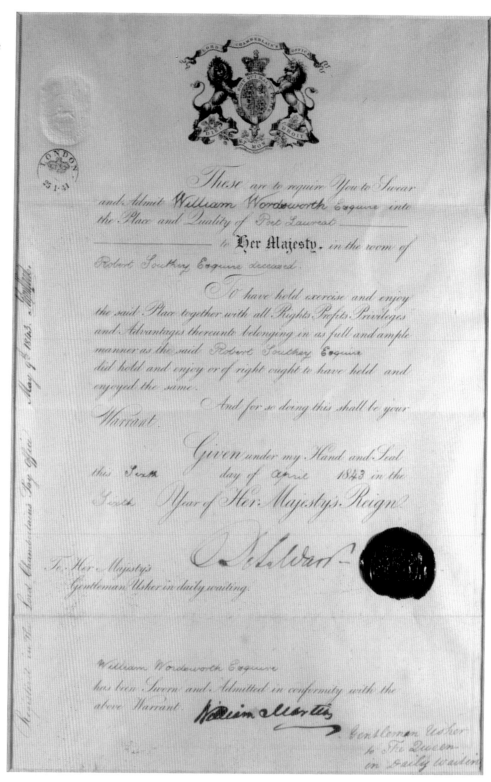

Rydal Mount: 1833-50

In the last years of his life Wordsworth finally achieved literary fame. *Yarrow Revisited and other Poems*, published in 1835, was his first genuinely popular work. In 1836-37 he worked on another collected edition of his works, in six volumes, and made his habitual painstaking revisions. The following year *The Sonnets of William Wordsworth* appeared, a deluxe volume containing some 415 examples of Wordsworth's favourite poetic form. His international profile was growing too, and he was particularly popular in America. In his final years Wordsworth also turned, once again, to the *Prelude*. He still considered the poem too personal to be published in his lifetime, but he revised it for publication after his death.

At Rydal Mount Wordsworth began to receive an enormous number of letters, gifts, and requests from unknown admirers and would-be poets. 'Do Pardon me, Sir', wrote a young Branwell Brontë from Yorkshire, 'that I have ventured to come before one whose works I have most loved in our Literature and who most has been with me a divinity of the mind – [for] laying before him one of my writings, and

William Westall's 1840 engraving of a room in Rydal Mount shows the Wordsworths as affluent and respectable in old-age.

Wordsworth Trust

William Wordsworth

Wordsworth's beloved daughter Dora, when she was thirty-five years old. Painting by Margaret Gillies, 1839.

108

asking of him a Judgement of its contents, – I must come before some one from whose sentence there is no appeal …' Others were determined to see the famous poet in person. These visitors (and the visitors book kept at Rydal Mount records many hundreds of them) ranged from the distinguished – Queen Adelaide of England, Ralph Waldo Emerson – to the tourist and souvenir hunter. Wordsworth, hardly less than the mountains and lakes themselves, was a part of the landscape.

With fame came official honours. In 1838 Wordsworth received an honorary degree at Durham University. The following year he was made an honorary doctor of civil law at Oxford. Finally, in 1843, following the death of Robert Southey, he was offered the Poet Laureateship. At first Wordsworth refused; he was, he said, too old. But when the prime minister, Sir Robert Peel, informed him that his appointment was the Queen's personal wish, he accepted. 'You shall have *nothing* required of you', Peel assured him.

But the centre of Wordsworth's existence remained his family, and here his final years were weighed down by anxiety and grief. His two surviving sons were finding it hard to live in their famous father's shadow. John, the eldest, had never been quick, and Wordsworth's attempt to act as his tutor had proved disastrous. Eventually, he settled down to a quiet life as a provincial clergyman. William, Wordsworth's other son, known in the family as Willy, never quite succeeded in finding his own place in life. After a period at Oxford University he drifted for some years, and Wordsworth despaired of him ever finding meaningful employment. Eventually he procured his son the post of sub-controller of stamps, and in 1842 Willy succeeded his father as Distributor.

Dora, Wordsworth's surviving daughter, was especially beloved. Hartley Coleridge had noticed how 'by the mere strength of affection she entered into the recesses of her father's mind and drew him out to gambol with her in the childishness that always hung upon her womanhood'. But Hartley saw it as an intense, and somewhat possessive love: 'strong indeed must be the love that could induce her to leave her father, whom she almost adores, and who quite doats upon her'. When, in 1838, Dora became engaged to Edward Quillinan, Wordsworth initially opposed the union – he considered a widower with an existing family and little prospects an unsuitable husband for his only daughter. He eventually gave his consent, and Dora

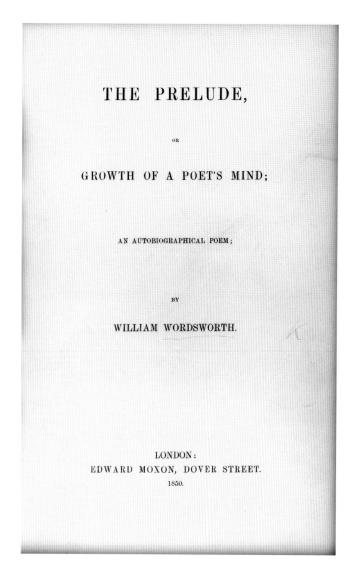

THE PRELUDE,

OR

GROWTH OF A POET'S MIND;

AN AUTOBIOGRAPHICAL POEM;

BY

WILLIAM WORDSWORTH.

LONDON:
EDWARD MOXON, DOVER STREET.
1850.

The Prelude *was published shortly after Wordsworth's death in 1850. Wordsworth never gave the poem a title, referring to it simply as 'the poem to Coleridge'. The title of 'The Prelude' was suggested by Mary Wordsworth.*

The British Library, 11645.f.5

and Quillinan were married in 1841, but tellingly, he was unable to attend the wedding, and Dora was given away by her brother William. Quillinan wrote to his daughter Rotha the following day:

Mr Wordsworth was so agitated at parting with his sole daughter that he said to me almost at the last moment, 'I have told Dora that I would accompany you to church if you wished it, but this interview with my child has already so upset me that I think I can hardly bear it.' We all then begged him not *to come, & it was agreed that his son William should act for him; but he gave us his blessing very affectionately both before & after the wedding: nothing could have been kinder than he & all have been.*

It was remarkably similar to a time almost forty years earlier, when Dorothy had been unable to witness Wordsworth's own marriage to Mary Hutchinson.

Dorothy, by this time, was a pale shadow of her former self. A serious illness in 1829 had left her in extreme pain. Further attacks, in 1831, 1833 and 1834 had broken her mental health. Now, the vivacious young woman of Dove Cottage, whose animated features De Quincey had so memorably described, had been reduced to a demented old woman who spent her days hunched over the fire in her room. Alcohol and opium were the only things that could relieve the constant pain, and Mary noticed how her strange behaviour 'would terrify strangers to death'. In fine weather, Wordsworth would wheel his 'dear ruin of a sister' round the garden at Rydal Mount.

As he worried about his family, the elderly Wordsworth watched old friends pass away one by one. Sir George Beaumont died in 1827 – 'nearly twenty-five years have I known him intimately', Wordsworth wrote to Samuel Rogers, 'and neither myself nor my family ever received a cold or unkind look from him'. Further losses followed: William Calvert in 1829, Sir Walter Scott in 1832, and James Losh in 1833. In 1834 he lost two particularly dear friends, Coleridge in July, and in December, Charles Lamb. Coleridge, Wordsworth said, was 'the most *wonderful* man that he had ever known'. A year later James Hogg died, and his death inspired Wordsworth to write one of his finest elegies, *Extempore Effusion upon the Death of James Hogg*. In the poem he remembers his departed friends. He thinks first of Coleridge,

> *The rapt One of the godlike forhead,*
> *The heaven-eyed creature sleeps in earth:*
> *And Lamb, the frolic and the gentle,*
> *Has vanished from his lonely hearth.*

> *Like clouds that rake the mountain-summits,*
> *Or waves that own no curbing hand,*
> *How fast has brother followed brother,*
> *From sunshine to sunless land!*

> *Yet I, who lids from infant slumber*
> *Were earlier roused, remain ro hear*
> *A timid voice, that asks in whispers,*
> *'Who next will drop and disappear?'*

But Wordsworth continued to form new friendships. Thomas Arnold, headmaster of Rugby School, had retired to the Lake District with his family, and lived at Fox How close to Rydal Mount. His son, Matthew Arnold, retained vivid memories of his visits to Rydal Mount, and later became one of Wordsworth's most perceptive champions. Perhaps dearest among these later friends was Isabella

Fenwick. Edward Quillinan wrote of her: 'Miss Fenwick is more than a favourite with Mr and Mrs Wordsworth, and I do not think they can now live in pefect ease without her. No wonder; she is a trump!' Miss Fenwick smoothed the way towards Dora's and Quillinan's marriage, and Wordsworth dictated to her a series of memoirs, the so-called 'Fenwick Notes', which together form an invaluable source of information about the the poet and his work.

In 1842 Wordsworth published *Poems, Chiefly of Early and Late Years*, which contained revised versions of his early works, 'Salisbury Plain' and 'The Borderers'. In 1844 he was roused to comment on a public matter, a proposed railway from Kendal to Windermere, which he considered invasive and passionately opposed. In 1845 he met the leading poet of the next generation, Alfred Tennyson, and pronouced him 'decidedly the first of our living poets'.

In July 1847 came the saddest death of all. Dora's health had been weak for some time, and in May 1845 she and Quillinan visited Portugal, where she seemed to benefit from the milder climate. On their return they settled in a house close to Rydal Mount, and in October the following year Wordsworth was describing his daughter to Isabella Fenwick as being 'wonderfully strong and well'. But that Christmas Dora caught a cold, and in the spring became dangerously ill. She was moved to Rydal Mount, and by May it was clear to everyone that she was dying. 'The voice is gone', Mary Wordsworth wrote to a friend on 7 May, 'the cough and perspirations encreased—but happily her *suffering* from the cough is not so tearing as it had been. Her mind is clear—and her heavenward aspirations are, I doubt not, *tho' in silence*, her support.' Five days later, at a quarter to one in the morning, Dora died. Wordsworth informed friends of her death in expressions of Christian stoicism, and appeared to be bearing up well to the tragedy. He devoted himself to caring for Dorothy. Privately, however, he was grief-stricken. He and his friend Henry Crabb Robinson went for walks every day, and afterwards, Mary Wordsworth said, 'he would retire to his room sit alone & cry incessantly'. 'She is ever with me', Wordsworth wrote to Isabella Fenwick in December, 'and will be so to the last moment of my life.'

For the next two years Wordsworth waited for that moment to come. In January 1849 Hartley Coleridge died. The day before the funeral Wordsworth and

Hartley's sister Sara walked over to Grasmere churchyard, where Dora had been laid to rest, and, years earlier, little Catherine and Thomas. There Hartley was now to be buried – 'Let him lie by us', Wordsworth told Sara, 'he would have wished it.' Then he asked the sexton to measure out the ground for his and Mary's own graves – 'Keep the ground for us', he said to the sexton, 'we are old people, and it cannot be long.'

The following March, Wordsworth took another walk to Grasmere. It was a cold evening, and two days later he fell ill with pleurisy. On 7 April he celebrated his eightieth birthday. Sixteen days later, on 23 April 1850, he died, as the cuckoo clock was striking the hours for noon.

The Wordsworth family graves in Grasmere churchyard. Dorothy lived for almost five years after her brother's death, dying on 25 January 1855. Mary Wordsworth died four years later, on 17 January 1859.

Alex Black

WILLIAM WORDSWORTH
1770-1850

⬦ *Chronology*

1770   William Wordsworth born on 7 April at Cockermouth.

1771   Dorothy Wordsworth born.

1778   Death of Wordsworth's mother, Ann.

1779   Wordsworth enters Hawkshead Grammar School.

1783   Death of Wordsworth's father, John.

1787   Wordsworth enters St John's College, Cambridge University.

1789   The Fall of the Bastille on 14 July.

1790   In the summer, goes on a walking tour with Robert Jones through France and Switzerland.

1791   Leaves Cambridge and spends time in London. In December he goes to France.

1792   In France, Wordsworth meets a revolutionary, Michel Beaupuy, and has a love affair with Annette Vallon. Their daughter, Caroline, is born in December. At the end of the year Wordsworth returns to London.

1793   France and Britain at war. Wordsworth publishes *An Evening Walk* and *Descriptive Sketches*, and writes *A Letter to the Bishop of Llandaff*, which is not published. He walks across Salisbury Plain then stays with Robert Jones in North Wales. Writes 'Salisbury Plain'.

1794   Wordsworth and Dorothy reunited at Windy Brow, Keswick. Wordsworth is bequeathed £900 by Raisley Calvert.

1795   Wordsworth goes to London and moves in radical circles. He meets William Godwin. In August he goes to Bristol and there meets Samuel Taylor Coleridge and Robert Southey. In September he and Dorothy go to live at Racedown Lodge in Dorset.

1797 Wordsworth writes *The Ruined Cottage* and completes a play, *The Borderers*. In June, Coleridge visits Racedown. In July, Wordsworth and Dorothy move to Alfoxden near Coleridge's home at Nether Stowey, Somerset. Intimate friendship begins between Wordsworth, Dorothy and Coleridge.

1798 Wordsworth and Coleridge both very productive. Wordsworth plans to write 'The Recluse'. Wordsworth and Dorothy leave Alfoxden and tour the Wye Valley. Wordsworth writes 'Tintern Abbey'. Wordsworth's and Coleridge's poetry is published anonymously in *Lyrical Ballads*. In September, Wordsworth, Dorothy and Coleridge go to Germany. Wordsworth and Dorothy winter at Goslar, and Wordsworth begins earliest version of *The Prelude*.

1799 Wordsworth and Dorothy return from Germany and stay with the Hutchinsons in the north east. In October, Wordsworth, Coleridge and Wordsworth's brother John tour the Lake District. In December, Wordsworth and Dorothy go to live at Dove Cottage in Grasmere.

1800 Coleridge comes to live in the Lake District. Wordsworth's brother John stays at Dove Cottage for most of the year.

1801 Second edition of *Lyrical Ballads* published in January, with additional poems and a preface written by Wordsworth in 1800.

1802 Wordsworth writes many poems. In August Wordsworth and Dorothy visit Annette and Caroline in France. In October Wordsworth marries Mary Hutchinson.

1803 First child, John is born. Wordsworth, Dorothy and Coleridge tour Scotland. Wordsworth meets Walter Scott.

1804 Coleridge, who has been ill, goes to Malta. Wordsworth's daughter, Dora is born. Works hard on *The Prelude* and completes 'Ode: Intimations of Immortality'.

1805 Wordsworth's brother John is drowned. Wordsworth completes *The Prelude*.

1806 Third child, Thomas is born. Wordsworth and family spend the winter at Coleorton, Leicestershire. They are reunited with Coleridge.

1807 *Poems in Two Volumes* published, to bad reviews.

1808 Wordsworth and family leave Dove Cottage for Allan Bank, also in Grasmere.

1809 Fourth child, Catherine is born. *The Convention of Cintra* is published.

1810 Fifth and final child, William is born. Wordsworth and Coleridge quarrel.

1811 Wordsworth and family move to Grasmere Parsonage.

1812 Wordsworth and Coleridge reconciled. Deaths of children, Catherine and Thomas.

1813 Wordsworth is appointed Distributor of Stamps for Westmorland. Family moves to Rydal Mount.

1814 Wordsworth tours Scotland with Mary. *The Excursion* is published, and attacked by reviewers.

1815 Publication of first Colleted Edition of poems, and *The White Doe of Rylestone*.

1817 Wordsworth meets Keats in London.

1818 Westmorland Election: Wordsworth campaigns for the Tories.

1819 Publication of *Peter Bell* and *The Waggoner*.

1820 Publication of the *River Duddon* sonnet sequence. Tour of Europe.

1822 *Memorials of a Tour on the Continent* and *Ecclesiastical Sketches* published.

1831 Wordsworth and Dora tour Scotland and see Walter Scott.

1834 Death of Coleridge.

1835 *Yarrow Revisited* published. Dorothy seriously ill. Beginning of her mental deterioration. Wordsworth writes 'Extempore Effusion upon the Death of James Hogg'.

1837 Tour of France and Italy.

1841 Dora marries Edward Quillinan.

1842 Wordsworth resigns as Distributor of Stamps. Publication of *Poems, Chiefly of Early and Late Years*.

1843 Wordsworth appointed Poet Laureate.

1847 Death of Dora Wordsworth.

1850 Wordsworth dies on 23 April. *The Prelude* published after his death.

❧ *Further Reading*

Original Works

The standard edition of Wordsworth's poetry is the *Cornell Wordsworth* (General Editor Stephen Parrish, Cornell University Press, 1975). There are also a number of selections, including:

William Wordsworth, from the Oxford Authors Series, ed. Stephen Gill (Oxford University Press, 1984)

William Wordsworth – An Illustrated Selection, ed. Jonathan Wordsworth (The Wordsworth Trust, 1987)

The Prelude – The Four Texts, ed. Jonathan Wordsworth (Penguin Books, 1995)

The standard edition of the letters is *The Letters of William and Dorothy Wordsworth* (ed. Ernest De Selincourt, rev. Alan G. Hill, Oxford 1967-93)

The standard edition of Dorothy Wordsworth's Grasmere Journals is *The Grasmere Journals* (ed. Pamela Woof, Oxford University Press, 1991)

Biographies

Hunter Davis, *William Wordsworth* (Sutton Publishing, 1997)

Stephen Gill, *William Wordsworth, A Life* (Clarenden Press, 1989)

Kenneth Johnston, *The Hidden Wordsworth* (W.W. Norton and Company, 1998)

Other Works

A.S. Byatt, *Unruly Times, Wordsworth and Coleridge in their Time* (Vintage, 1997)

Stephen Gill, *Wordsworth and the Victorians* (Clarenden Press, 1998)

Pamela Woof, *Dorothy Wordsworth Writer* (The Wordsworth Trust, 1994)

Robert Woof and Stephen Hebron, *Towards Tintern Abbey* (The Wordsworth Trust, 1998)

Jonathan Wordsworth, Michael C. Jaye and Robert Woof, *William Wordsworth and the Age of English Romanticism* (Rutgers University Press, 1987)

◀ *Index*

Alfoxden, 39-40

Allan Bank, 81, 82, 85, 86

Arnold, Matthew, 111

Arnold, Thomas, 111

Bastille, 19, 24

Beaumont, Sir George, 69, 73, 75, 76, 86, 93, 111

Beaupuy, Michel, 25-6

Bristol, 24, 46

Brontë, Branwell, 107-9

Byron, Lord, 78, 95

Calvert, Raisley, 31, 33, 53

Calvert, William, 30, 31, 111

Cambridge, 16-17, 23, 25

Clarkson, Catherine, 54, 58, 85, 86, 90, 102

Clarkson, Thomas, 54, 58, 102

Cockermouth, 7, 9, 13

Coleridge, Hartley, 38, 39, 62, 76, 81, 104, 109, 112, 113

Coleridge, Samuel Taylor, 34, 35, 36 *passim*; moves to
    Keswick, 58; goes to Malta, 69; returns to
    England, 76; at Allan Bank, 81-5; quarrels with
    Wordsworth, 86; death, 111

Coleridge, Sara, 82, 112-13

Cottle, Joseph, 35, 48, 53, 54

De Quincey, Thomas, 79, 81, 82-3, 87, 110

Dove Cottage, 54, 56 *passim*

Edridge, Henry, 74

Fenwick, Isabella, 111-12

Fox, Charles James, 61, 74

Godwin, William, 28, 33, 74

Goslar, 49-52

Grasmere, 55 *passim*, 90

Grasmere Rectory, 86, 88

Gray, Thomas, 20, 55

Hamburg, 49

Hamilton, William Rowan, 102

Hawkshead, 9-15, 17, 25

Haydon, Benjamin Robert, 96, 102, 104

Hazlitt, William, 45-6, 94-5, 96

Hogg, James, 90-1, 111

Hutchinson, Sara, 58, 62, 66-7, 81, 83, 85-6, 87, 100

Jeffrey, Francis, 78, 94

Johnson, Joseph, 28

Jones, Robert, 18-23, 31, 58, 100, 102

Keats, John, 96-7

Klopstock, Wilhelm, 49

Lamb, Charles, 36, 39, 74, 102, 111

Losh, James, 33, 44, 58, 111

Lowther, Sir James, 7, 15, 89

Lowther, Sir William, 89, 90, 93, 102

Montagu, Basil (senior), 33, 36, 53, 74, 86

Montagu, Basil (junior), 33, 36

Pinney, John and Azariah, 33, 35

Poole, Thomas, 39, 53, 67, 83

Quillinan, Edward, 102, 109-10, 112

Racedown Lodge, 33, 34, 38
'Rock of Names', 62
Rydal Mount, 90

Salisbury Plain, 30
Scott, Walter, 67-9, 102, 104, 110
Shelley, Percy Bysshe, 90, 95-6
Southey, Robert, 34, 37, 53, 87, 94, 109

Tennyson, Alfred, 112
Thelwall, John, 33, 40-2
Tintern Abbey, 46, 48
Tyson, Ann, 10-11

Vallon, Annette, 26-7, 63, 100
Vallon, Caroline, 27, 63, 100

Wordsworth, Ann (mother), 7, death of, 9
Wordsworth, Catherine, 81, death of, 87
Wordsworth, Christopher (brother), 7, 102
Wordsworth, Dora (daughter), 71, 102, 109-10, death of, 112
Wordsworth, Dorothy, 7, 9, 15, 19, 20, 23, 31, 34 *passim*; Alfoxden Journal, 42; Grasmere Journal, 58-9; illness, 110
Wordsworth, John (father), 7, 12, death of, 13-15
Wordsworth, John (brother), 7, 54, 58, 62, death of, 71-3, 74, 75
Wordsworth, John (son), 67, 109
Wordsworth (née Hutchinson), Mary (wife), 15, 36, 39, 46, 52, 58, 62, 63-6, 79
Wordsworth, Thomas (son), 76, death of, 87, 88

Wordsworth, William
Life: Early childhood, 7-9; school at Hawkshead, 9-15; at Cambridge, 16-23; tour of the Alps, 18-23; in France, 24-7; in London, 28-9; in Keswick, 31; in Dorset, 34-8; in Somerset, 39-48; in Germany, 49-52; at Dove Cottage, 55-79; marriage, 63-6; at Allan Bank, 81-6; at Rydal Mount, 88-113; death, 113
Works: *An Evening Walk*, 18, 28, 31; 'The Borderers', 36, 38; *Convention of Cintra*, 82-3; *Descriptive Sketches*, 28; 'Duddon Sonnets', 98-9; *Ecclesiastical Sketches*, 101; 'Elegiac Stanzas', 75; 'Essays upon Epitaphs', 83-5; *The Excursion*, 91-3, 94, 96; 'Extempore Effusion upon the Death of James Hogg', 111; *Guide to the Lakes*, 85; 'Home at Grasmere', 55-6, 93; 'A Letter to the Bishop of Llandaff', 28-9; *Lyrical Ballads* (1798), 44-5, 47-48, 53; *Lyrical Ballads* (1800), 59-61, 78; 'Michael', 60-1; 'Ode: Intimations of Immortality', 62, 69; 'Peter Bell', 45, 96-9; *Poems in Two Volumes*, 78-9; *The Prelude*, 20, 45, 51-2, 69-71, 73, 78, 92, 107; 'The Recluse', 44, 70, 86, 91-2, 100; 'Reply to Mathetes', 83; 'Resolution and Independence', 62-3; 'The Ruined Cottage', 38, 43-4; 'Salisbury Plain', 30, 35-6; 'Surprised by Joy', 87; 'Tintern Abbey', 46-7; 'The Vale of Esthwaite', 15; *The White Doe of Rylestone*, 93; 'Yarrow Revisited', 105-6
Wordsworth, William (son), 86, 109

The British Library is grateful to the Wordsworth Trust, the Birmingham Museum and Art Gallery, Musées de la Ville, Paris, the Trustees of the National Portrait Gallery, the National Trust, Norwich Museums Service and other named copyright holders for permission to reproduce illustrations.

Front cover illustrations: William Wordsworth by Henry Edridge (Wordsworth Trust); 'At Vallombrosa', The British Library Ashley MS 4645 f.1; Grasmere by Fennel Robson (Wordsworth Trust)

Back cover illustrations: William Wordsworth by W.H. Pickersgill (Wordsworth Trust); Dove Cottage (Wordsworth Trust)

Half-title page: Wordsworth Trust (Wordsworth Trust)

Frontispiece: Printer's instructions for *Poems in two volumes*, 1807, The British Library Additional MS 47864 f.3

Contents page: Dove Cottage, (Wordsworth Trust):

Text copyright: © 2000 Stephen Hebron
Illustrations copyright: © 2000 The British Library Board, Wordsworth Trust, and other named copyright holders

Published in the United States of America by
Oxford University Press, Inc.
198 Madison Avenue
New York, NY 10016
www.oup.com

Oxford is a registered trademark of Oxford University Press, Inc.

ISBN 0-19-521560-5

First published 2000 by The British Library, 96 Euston Road, London NW1 2DB

Designed and typeset by Crayon Design, Stoke Row, Henley-on-Thames
Map by John Mitchell
Colour origination by Crayon Design and South Sea International Press
Printed in Hong Kong by South Sea International Press